Home Ec

Focus on . . .

Adding Eye Appeal to Foods

Focus on...
The Hospitality Industry
by Bruce H. Axler

Adding Eye Appeal to Foods
Breakfast Cookery
Building Care for Hospitality Operations
Buying and Using Convenience Foods
Increasing Lodging Revenues and Restaurant Checks
Kitchen Sanitation and Food Hygiene
Practical Wine Knowledge
Profitable Catering
Room Care for Hotels and Motels
Security for Hotels, Motels, and Restaurants
Showmanship in the Dining Room
Tableservice Techniques

ITT Educational Publishing
Indianapolis · New York

Focus on...

Adding Eye Appeal to Foods

by
Bruce H. Axler

Noted
Food Educator
and Consultant

ITT EDUCATIONAL
PUBLISHING
INDIANAPOLIS • NEW YORK

Adding Eye Appeal to Foods

Copyright © 1974 by Howard W. Sams & Co., Inc.

All rights reserved

> No part of this book may be reproduced or transmitted in any form or by any means, electronic or mechanical, including photocopying, recording, or by any information storage and retrieval system, without permission in writing from Howard W. Sams & Co., Inc., 4300 West 62nd Street, Indianapolis, Indiana 46268.

Library of Congress Cataloging in Publication Data

Axler, Bruce H.
  Adding eye appeal to foods.

  (His Focus on . . . the hospitality industry)
  At head of title: Focus on . . .
  1. Cookery for institutions, etc. 2. Cookery
(Garnishes) 3. Food service I. Title.
TX820.A93   641.5'7   74–8644
ISBN 0–672–26115–4

Printed in the United States of America

1. 9 8 7 6 5 4 3 2 1

Book design, cover design, and cover illustration by Jorge Hernandez.

Contents

Showmanship on the Plate / **1**
    Eye Appeal for Every Operation   2
    Starting a Food Showmanship Program   4
    Taste, Gimmicks, Clichés, and the
        Art of Decoration   5

The Art of Making Food Attractive / **2**
    Using Color   9
    Using Texture and Form   12
    Plate Composition   16

Accessories / **3**
    Specialty Serviceware   22
    Disposable Accessorization   26
    Decorative Treatments   26

Eye Appeal for Quantity
Food Presentation / **4**
    Dining Room Displays   29
    Eye Appeal in Cafeteria Service   32

Eye Appeal for Buffets / **5**
    Arrangement of the Buffet in the Room   40
    Nonedible Decoration   42
    Major Pieces   46

Platter Decoration	51
Arrangement of the Buffet	59

Eye Appeal for Salads / 6
Main Salad Elements	62
Garnish Elements	69
Assembling Salads	71

Eye Appeal for Cold Plates / 7
Garnishes and Decoration	75
Plate Composition	86

Eye Appeal for Sandwiches / 8
Types of Sandwiches	89
Decorations and Garnishes for Sandwiches	97

Eye Appeal for Hot Foods / 9
Selectivity in the Choice of Items	99
Proper Preparation	100
Strong Accessorization	101
Eye-Arresting Garnishes	101
Finishing Touches	103

Eye Appeal for Cakes, Desserts, and Beverages / 10
Cakes	105
Desserts	107
Beverages	109

Showmanship on the Plate

Any restaurateur can make dollar profits at a cost of pennies per plate.

People tend to eat with their eyes. Give them food, and if they like the looks of it, they'll like the taste of it. They'll like the restaurant, and they'll come back for more.

The dramatic four-color, full-spread photos of food appearing in magazines have set visual standards for the restaurateur. If he can make his food look that mouth-watering, it will be irresistible to his guests. If it is any less luscious looking, it suffers by comparison to such photos; especially when the guest has had three ice-cold dry martinis and cannot really taste the difference between a prickly pear and a mashed rutabaga.

Without substantial expense or labor, cold ingredients artfully arranged become chef's creations; attractively garnished plates become house specialties; and dramatic desserts become high-profit volume sellers.

The thought, care, and taste that was lavished on an operation's decor, furnishings, and serviceware should be applied to its food. The big profits are in the big picture: beautiful place, beautiful table, beautiful food.

Adding Eye Appeal to Foods systematically discusses how to make food look attractive and appetizing—how to make platters, hors d'oeuvres, cold dishes, salads, hot entrées, desserts, and beverages look great. In addition to a unique collection of decorative effects, the book offers guidelines for using color and texture, composing plates and platters, and accessorizing dishes, in order to give each food its maximum appeal.

The right use of color makes 10¢ worth of ice cream a dollar confection. The right presentation and garnishes make yesterday's leftover tonight's $8 special. The right plate look makes a 12-ounce steak give 16 ounces of pleasure.

Eye Appeal for Every Operation

Precisely because attractive food is only a matter of taste and attention—not dependent on food cost, labor cost, or service—it can be served in any operation. Some fast food dishes are among the most appealing. Few dishes in expensive restaurants have the visual appeal of triple-decker hamburgers, fish 'n' chips, pizza, overstuffed sandwiches on French bread, or, for that matter, a banana split.

If we analyze these simple but attractive items—or other, more sophisticated dishes that have visual appeal—we find that certain identifiable elements contribute to their charm:

1. The dish itself is a "composition"—it has unity and wholeness.
2. There is good use of color—a single appealing color, complementary colors, or contrasting colors.
3. Texture is used to good visual advantage: Shapes and forms contrast with other shapes and forms. The banana split and the hamburger are excellent examples.
4. The relationship of the food and whatever it is served on is pleasing; it fills the plate (or whatever) attractively.
5. The purchaser or consumer can easily recognize what the food is.

Other qualities are also important—drama, "fun" accessorization—but these five are usually noticeable by their absence in food served in restaurants, from the smallest diner to the best hotel dining room.

As examples of poor planning, some of the best restaurants serve all brown dinners (and in bad light at that): brown sauce, brown meat, brown potatoes, and brown vegetables au gratin. Cafeterias have mastered the art of uniform presentation: Everything possible is portioned with an ice cream scoop. Coffee shops serve sandwiches that seem to have crash landed on the plate. Buffets are loaded with mystery meats and salads similarly garnished with parsley and rouged with paprika like so many ancient chorines.

Several factors have contributed to the continuing poor appearance of food. It has been possible for restaurateurs to serve so much food that quantity almost made up for the lack of quality and appeal. Customers were less demanding; they ate just to fill themselves up.

Nowadays, food is too expensive for the restaurateur to afford the price of overwhelming the customer, and the customer is demanding much more than a full stomach. He wants a total experience: the taste of food, the smell of food, and the pleasant anticipation stimulated by its visual appeal.

Any restaurateur who examines his offerings and then his operation will find that there is no excuse for any dish looking as if it came out of a doggie bag. It costs very little more, if anything, to make a dish look appetizing, and it may mean added profits.

The solution, of course, is to look at a plate—any plate, any dish—as the customer sees it. Which is more appealing, the dry breakfast cereal in the box in a china bowl, or the dry breakfast cereal out of the box in a high or footed glass bowl? Which is more appealing, a plate awash in chicken à la king or the chicken à la king in a pastry shell or yellow rice ring? Which is more appealing, a closed ham and cheese sandwich, seemingly cut in two with a hatchet, or the same sandwich, open-faced, with overlapping rolls of ham and cheese on one side of the bread and the tomato slices shingled on a lettuce leaf on the other side?

Starting a Food Showmanship Program

It is sometimes difficult for a restaurateur to examine his menu items objectively: He knows too much about them to actually see them with the customer's perspective. Yet obviously he must examine them critically to make them more appealing. Color photographs of his food offer the restaurateur one of the most effective ways of gaining a new perspective. Even self-developing pictures, which make all food—including attractive food—look bad, allow the restaurateur to quickly identify the problems.

Away from the restaurant, he can shuffle through the pictures and begin to notice that he cannot easily identify some of the food items. Others look as though the choice of serving vessel was made by lot. Some plates look virtually naked. Viewing the pictures can help him identify some major problems—he may see that the money he is putting into the item is not apparent, or that a little upgrading could make a big difference in selling price and appeal. He may find, for example, that his really great beef burgundy looks like mulligan stew or it will occur to him that a mere scoop of mashed potatoes has the potential to become a golden brown rosette or duchess potatoes.

Such foods are prime targets for the restaurateur's attention because, one way or another, there is a profit in improving them. Perhaps the beef burgundy needs an individual casserole; an attractively shaped, fried crouton half dipped in chopped parsley; or glazed boiled onions instead of plain boiled onions—or all three. The answer soon becomes apparent with a little experimentation after the restaurateur overcomes the major obstacle: posing the question.

As a start, some general questions might be suggested:

1. What is it—vegetable soup or clam chowder? If it looks like vegetable soup, how can the customer be made to see that it's "Manhattan Clam Chowder, chock full of tender, juicy Long Island clams" as the menu promises?
2. Does anyone want to eat it the way it looks? Is it unappetizing—does it look as though somebody had already eaten it and didn't like it?
3. Does it look worth the menu price? How can it be made to seem like a good value for the money? A lobster tail in the shell doesn't look like very much; a lobster tail on top of the shell does.
4. What would it take to make this item worth 20 percent more? It might be 2¢ worth of grated cheese or 3¢ worth of anchovies.
5. Why use that particular vessel for that dish? Who decided on it? For example, the standard convenience chicken cordon bleu barely dirties a coupe-shaped 10-inch dinner plate. Serve it on a smaller plate? Or add a garnish that covers the plate?

Taste, Gimmicks, Clichés, and the Art of Decoration

Food itself is beautiful. It only has to be high-lighted and complemented to be attractive. Cooks who tend toward overdecoration, rococo effects, and cuteness make food as appetizing as a glass that has just been emptied of buttermilk. They miss the mark as widely as those chefs who belong to the order-of-the-lemon-wedge or the sprig-of-watercress fraternity. Modern taste is pleased by artful embellishment and elaboration that strike a medium somewhere between a dash of paprika and a re-creation of the Battle of Waterloo in chopped liver. Simplicity and naturalness are the keys. Some basic rules can be formulated for treatments that have the most appeal (and profit potential) without turning the meal into a menagerie of vegetable animals or a culinary art salon.

1. See a dish as the customer sees it. Consider the taste of the market, the type of customer, the hour of the day, the type of service personnel, the dining room decor, the lighting, and so on.
2. Maximize the attractiveness of the food itself.
3. Strive for very simple visual statements—light, elegant touches instead of massive, complex constructions.
4. Don't overwhelm the main item with garnish.
5. Avoid inedible garnishes that look like food.
6. Think about the appearance of the food as it is eaten or served.
7. Avoid representational effects: bunny rabbits of mashed potatoes, pigs made out of lemons, penguins made from hard-cooked eggs.
8. Use the plate, platter, or tray as a frame; respect its borders.
9. Make sure that the garnish or decorative elements complement the flavor of the food as well as its appearance.
10. Be neat.

In addition to the pleasure of the diner, the application of these rules has a further dividend: the limitation of operational problems. If the restaurateur knows how he wants his food to look, he can acquire the elements that will make it attractive for a few cents —or less. Only classically trained chefs can create architectural masterpieces. But after a moment's instruction, any cook capable of cooking green beans is capable of sprinkling them with toasted sesame seeds (for texture interest, color contrast, taste, and more novelty than almonds).

Naturalistic, tasteful decoration is especially suited to convenience foods. On the one hand, a convenience item requires custom decoration, accessorization, or garnishing, or it will look like the same dish everybody else is serving. On the other hand, the problem of finding and being able to afford the master chefs capable of elaborate dishes prompted the use of convenience foods in the first place. Whoever cooks them or heats them can make convenience foods attractive. Just consider that classic convenience food, ice cream, and the artistic creations (from prepared products) that every high school soda jerk is capable of producing after three days on the job. What he does with whipped cream, maraschino cherries, and crushed pineapple, the minimally skilled worker in the kitchen or the pantry can do with pickles, nuts, canned fruits and vegetables, bits of salad, and so on—still for pennies a plate.

2

The Art of Making Food Attractive

Whoever designs a dish has concerns similar to those of the artist in any plastic medium. Although it would be dangerous to extend the comparison too far since differences in the problems are equally apparent, the designer of a dish, like the painter, has to work with color, texture, and form. Each has to use these elements to create a pleasing design within a definite space—the canvas or the plate. The restaurateur or the chef has something to learn from the contemporary creative artist's control of color, exploitation of texture, and sense of composition.

The food designer has extensive opportunities for creation. Foods are available to him in infinite hues for use as both main elements and garnishes. Sharp knives, special devices, and even mechanical cutters give him control over a food's texture and form. He can choose to use a plate that provides a neutral background of polished white china, or he can compose his design on specialty dishes in a wide variety of colors, textures, and forms.

Given a sense of what he is doing and why he is doing it, the restaurateur—even one who does not cook or the chef himself can create attractive, pleasure-producing, arresting dishes.

Using Color

Roles of Color in Creating Eye Appeal

If a pleasing dish is analyzed carefully, it becomes evident that color plays three important roles in the design:

1. It has been used to interrupt the visual monotone boredom of the dish.
2. Some important element has been highlighted.
3. Color has been used to bring some pleasant association to the viewer's mind—perhaps an association with the taste of the food, perhaps an association with good times.

The most frequent use of color is to relieve an otherwise monotone dish. The natural color of many cooked and uncooked foods is pleasant enough, but boring. The brown of well-cooked meats, the orange of carrots, and the green of lettuce are all quite pleasing, but each requires a touch of some contrasting color to call attention to its attractiveness. Otherwise, there is too much brown, orange, or green for the viewer to see it as pretty at all.

On the other hand, some monotone foods are not attractive by themselves. The added colorful element gives them their only interest. For example, white sauce is hardly thrilling. Adding some colorful element such as chopped pimiento or the brown crust of an au gratin makes it begin to look like food for people.

When an item is actually ugly, color is a necessary mask. Stewed lamb, for example, is not anyone's idea of a visual treat, but if the pale grayish meat with scraps of off-yellow fat is put in a bright yellow curry or hidden in a mosaic of vegetables in a lamb stew, it looks good.

A color highlight should be placed where the viewer's attention should be focused. A cherry on top of a colorful parfait accentuates the height of the parfait. A dot of truffle or black olive in the middle of a colorful open-faced sandwich causes the viewer to look at its colorful elements.

Color can be very effectively exploited for the associations it offers. Certainly associations with sense of taste and touch are first. Blue, for example, is identified with cold; it's wrong for mashed potatoes but right for a frozen dessert. Red is hot, spicy, and rich. White is bland. Dark green is crisper than light green.

Dark shades of a color are richer and more flavorful than light shades, but dark meat is tougher than light meat. Few cooks are reluctant to augment the color of a brown stew with some carmelized sugar or the commercial products that contain it. Nor do they hesitate to add food coloring to pea soup or a yellow tinge to hollandaise sauce or mayonnaise.

Color is quite important when it is directly associated with the way a food tastes. An orange seems to taste juicier and sweeter if it is bright orange rather than an uncertain yellow-orange. A peach with a blush of red over a large part of its surface seems better than a yellow one. Somehow a green ripe apple never seems as sweet as a red one.

Color can also have more abstract associations. They can be as simple as the association of green with freshness and naturalness or as sophisticated as the association of yellow, red, and green with Mexican food, and, by extension, with fiestas, fun, and gaiety.

On a practical basis, then, color can tell the viewer/diner that he can anticipate a chilled, crisp salad, a velvety rich sauce, a hearty cup of soup, a spicy dish of rice, or a rich, sweet chocolate dessert. By way of negative proof, try changing the color of any food, and test the reactions to the changes. For instance, put a few drops of green food color in a glass of orange juice or a few drops of blue in a glass of milk.

Exploiting Color

In an actual restaurant kitchen, the exploitation of color for visual appeal can include the abundant use of foods with pleasing natural color, the free use of easy-to-add colorful elements, and the creation of dishes with definite color schemes.

Some foods have very pleasing natural colors. Proper cooking techniques maximize their attractiveness: foods fried golden brown, meats roasted and lacquered to a deep brown by their own juices and basting, green vegetables prevented from turning olive black, red—not purple—cabbage, and so on.

In addition to curly parsley, which is attractive but overused, the cook has a magnificent collection of colorful elements available to him. Red, yellow, and blue food colors—either liquids or pastes—tastefully give color to soups, sauces, and desserts. More exotic sources of the same colors, such as pomegranate seeds for red or kumquats for yellow-orange, provide additional dimensions.

Using color schemes for dishes offers creative opportunities for making food attractive; however, it also presents additional problems. The garnish element must coordinate well with the dish. The restaurateur might look to the cuisines of other countries for inspiration—tasty and colorful combinations of meats and vegetables; starches, meats, and fruits; or greens garnishing cooked dishes. Even if the operation cannot include these exact dishes in the menu, the lesson in the use of color is adaptable to what can be served. For example, green and yellow squash work with lamb; hard-cooked eggs and olives work with meat loaf. Any international cookbook has dozens of good examples of colorful dishes, among them Spanish paella, Japanese sukiyaki, French bouillabaisse, Argentine carbonado, Turkish kebabs, and Spanish and Mexican stews (cocido).

Using Texture and Form

Texture and form can be used effectively to increase food's attractiveness. Take macaroni, for example. Although there are only slight differences in ingredients among macaroni products, there are tremendous differences in their appearance: shells, bowties, ricelike grains, long strings, hollow tubes, and so on. Using a more exotic shape makes a new dish out of an old favorite. Frozen potatoes for frying offer the same kind of variety in form and texture without actually changing anything else: shoestring, steakhouse, crinkle cut, and French fry are just a few of the many kinds available.

The restaurateur's systematic attention to texture and form as visual elements can offer nearly effortless dividends. For example, an operation that uses sheet cakes has the choice of cutting them into squares, which tells everyone that they are sheet cakes, or cutting them first into strips and then into diagonal cuts which makes them seem like pieces of "home style" round cakes.

The mere consideration of texture and form as important elements in food appeal can have positive results. Should the potato salad resemble cold mashed potatoes, or should the customer be allowed to see definite quarter-sized pieces of potato? Should he be served elegant, cigar-shaped omelets or griddle-style pancakes? Would he rather see butter chips, butter balls, or butter in small, individual pots? Oval or round hamburger steaks?

Exploiting Natural Texture and Form

Some foods have visually pleasing textures and forms. They can give interest and appeal to items that are not themselves very attractive. Most of these items, among scores of others, can be used with very little extra work:

1. Twists made from slices of citrus fruit
2. Sliced or split stuffed green olives
3. Coconut shred as topping for main dishes with sweet sauces
4. Deep-fried, precooked macaroni products of all types as topping for main dishes and in salads
5. Curly greens such as parsley, watercress, mint, kale, and chickory
6. Pickles
7. Sliced scallions
8. Slivered, chopped, halved, or whole nuts
9. Capers
10. Quality canned fruits

Other foods virtually stand alone, and altering their texture and form is a mistake. Here are some common errors: Salads are crushed, with two results—it takes more salad to fill a bowl, and the attractive, fresh spring is lost. Celery, chives, and mushrooms are chopped instead of sliced. Pie fillings, instead of being firm, are reduced to sweet mushiness.

Modifying Texture and Form

In many circumstances, the texture and form of the finished product depends on how the raw ingredients were cut and with what utensils. All food operations modify the texture and form of some raw ingredients; for most restaurants increasing the appeal of foods through texture and form is only a matter of introducing new cuts and tools. In volume operations, which are essentially limited to using mechanical devices that either slice or chop, the management can at least decide which cut is more appropriate for each food served. The decision can make a substantial difference in the final product: sliced or "grated" coleslaw as opposed to chopped coleslaw; shredded lettuce for sandwiches or whole lettuce leaves; chopped apple pie filling or sliced apple pie filling; and so on.

Operations that can afford some labor involvement can take advantage of the extra appeal that results from using a multitude of devices and special cutters. Most of these tools have been used in commercial operations only by classical decorators, even though they are readily available and inexpensive and require no special skills.

> Potato and melon scoops Hemispheres of stainless steel on handles, ranging in size from half a pea to half a golf ball, used to make balls of melons, turnips, carrots, and so on. Other shapes have been manufactured, notably several sizes of half an olive with and without fluting, but these are rare.
>
> Butter curler A sharp hook of flexible metal in a handle, used to make curls from blocks of butter.
>
> Butter paddles Small wooden paddles with a grooved surface and a flat surface. Hard butter is scooped with a potato scoop and then rolled in the paddles to produce elegant balls. Especially attractive with flavored or colored butters.
>
> Lemon zester A kind of peeler with small eyelets that remove strips of lemon, orange, or grapefruit peel.
>
> Lemon stripper or channel cutter A tiny knife edge cuts a shallow 3/16-inch strip from citrus fruits, melons, cucumbers, and so on for notched slices and decorative crisscrossing. Left-handed, right-handed, and vertical versions are available.
>
> Mandoline or Mar-For (a brand name that has

become generic) A relatively expensive ($10 to $30, depending on material) hand device that cuts potato chips and julienne potatoes and waffle weaves vegetables.

Vegetable decorating knife A paring knife with a serrated side (not edge) for turning vegetables and making decorative cuts.

Egg slicer Cuts hard-cooked, peeled eggs into slices.

Egg wedger Cuts hard-cooked eggs into six wedges or allows the cook to make a "daisy" by not completing the cut.

Nesting potato baskets The classic nesting baskets produce a fried potato "nest" about the size of a cup from parcooked shredded potatoes. Several manufacturers make other shapes and sizes.

Pastry wheels For trimming, sealing, and finishing dough edges, and also for "fluting" cheese strips and other soft, flat items.

Serrator A food "chopper" with a serrated (notched) edge to give firm vegetables, like potatoes or carrots, a crinkle cut.

Cutters Sets of cutters, similar to cookie cutters but of higher quality and in a wider variety of shapes and sizes, are used to create many of the decorative effects people admire in culinary shows. Round (column), round fluted, oval plain, oval fluted, specialty shapes for canapés or sandwiches, heart-shaped, and star-shaped are among the sets available.

Molds It is standard practice to use molds to form cakes and pastries. Hot dishes—for example, fish mousse—can also be molded in simple geometric or decorative shapes or representational forms. Any restaurant supply store offering utensils for quality baking has hundreds of different metal molds. Round or conical ice cream scoops are types of molds, too, and molds are also available in wood for butter.

Specialty cutters   The gadgetry with which housewives amuse themselves has its parallel in professional tools. For example, two knife-sharp rings on a metal screw, called a potato curler, cut a double helix that can be unwound from potatoes and carrots. The "radish cutter" reduces a radish, or a piece of any vegetable about the same size and texture, into a long, elegant spiral. There are a number of other tools with unusual shapes. The results are often charming and the customer has difficulty figuring out the method of cutting.

Strainers and ricers   Ricers and spaetzle makers are two of a number of devices that change the form of soft foods.

Pastry bags and tubes   Pastry bags can be fitted with any of about one hundred different standard tubes that allow the food in the bag—mashed potatoes, butter, or icing—to be extruded in some definite shape. Even simple rosettes made with a star tube add considerable visual appeal to any kind of pureed item.

Plate Composition

Both attractive and ordinary foods become more appealing when they are well arranged. As most service in the United States uses plates, rather than platters or wagons, the plate becomes the unit of design. The restaurateur or the chef asks himself how the food will look on the plate, how the customer will see it. Food items—main elements, vegetables, starches, and garnishes—are seen in relation to each other in the space defined by the plate. Their colors and textures are coordinated into a composition.

The restaurateur also has some control over the contribution of the plate to the design: He can decide on plate size, shape, and color.

Before the restaurateur can even consider upgrading the appearance of his plates by better coordination of the food elements on them, he must address himself to some often-neglected basics. The plate itself must be clean and unmarked. Excellent composition can be neutralized by bits of food matter that have not been washed from the plate by the dish machine, by the bluish-grey streaks caused by contact of the plate with soft metal, or by patches of worn miffle (glaze).

Sloppy portioning is another fundamental problem. Often the plate is spattered with food by the cook or sloshed by the waiter. Drippings on the outside of a bowl, for example, detract considerably from the food design on the inside and, of course, from the overall appearance of the dish.

Types of Plates

There are four basic shapes of standard plates: round, oval, square, and rectangular. Different rims offer the restaurateur further variations: wide rim, narrow rim, narrow rim scalloped, and coupe (rimless). In designing the dish, the restaurateur should also consider the depth of the plate and its overall size.

Even without consideration of design or color, these variables offer a large number of alternatives if the restaurateur has a design in mind. If he has a plate and an item but no design, the plate determines at least the outlines of the design. For example, a deep, wide-rim dish requires an arrangement that will make the portion look adequate, because these plate characteristics reduce the apparent size of portions. A coupe-shaped dish (without a rim) suggests the use of garnish elements that will cover the plate. Long items look better on rectangular or oval plates. Square dishes nicely "frame" elaborately composed dishes.

Often convenience items such as preportioned steaks or chicken cordon bleu are difficult to present well. Half a broiled chicken covers more than half of the standard 11-inch dinner plate, and the dish can be well arranged by adding a vegetable or even just a starch and a garnish. However, on the wrong 11-inch plate, the chicken cordon bleu or preportioned steak is lost. Unless the operator is willing to buy a new plate or load the plate with garnish, he should use the luncheon plate in the same service for such entrées.

Plate Arrangement

To arrange plates attractively the restaurateur or chef must first consider them from the diner's physical perspective. Unlike the man who may be standing at a work table as he arranges the plate, the diner is seated before it. There are two major differences: (1) He no longer sees it as a full circle; to him it has a back and a front—that is, a near side and a far side; (2) He is aware of its height, but the man arranging the plate is looking down on it and is not.

The implications of these differences are important. Consider a symmetrical design on a round plate—for example, a salad of crab meat precisely in the middle of radiating spokes of chopped hard egg, grated carrot, diced green pepper, and tomato wedges in a border of leaf lettuce. Looking down on the plate, there is an attractive symmetrical floral design. The crab meat is clearly the focus and the most important element.

Looking across the plate from the diner's perspective, much of the attractiveness is lost. One of the vegetable elements is directly in front of the diner;

another cannot really be seen completely. The focus has switched away from the crab meat and has been diffused. To make the plate attractive, the back has to be clearly established with the lettuce, the crab meat has to be placed forward of the center of the plate and bracketed by the garnishes. In other words, the salad has to be built, not simply laid out.

Principles of Arrangement

The principles of attractive plate arrangement can be summarized in a few easy-to-apply guidelines:

1. Establish a back and a front to the plate; build from the back to the front. Left-right symmetry is not necessary; left-right balance is.
2. Make sure that one point on the plate is the focus, but not necessarily the physical center.
3. Vary the height of the food items so that the plate has three definite dimensions. Mounds are better than blobs, rolls better than slices, shingled layers better than piles, and so on.
4. Vary the form and texture of the items. Avoid three mounds, three circles, all squares, or all cubes, and so on.
5. Place items with contrasting colors next to each other; separate similarly colored items.
6. Use the rim of the plate or an even border of the plate as a frame and keep the food in the well. When something extends beyond the border, make the effect a dramatic accent.
7. Make the arrangement simple, using as few elements as possible to make a pleasing composition that will cover the plate.
8. Arrange the food so that the eye travels into the plate, not away from it, following lines made by the food. The bones of chops, for example, can point in and up rather than down and out.

9 Place larger, heavier-appearing items on the inside of the composition and lighter pieces on the outside.
10 Use an odd number whenever possible—three, five, or seven pieces of vegetable rather than four, six, or eight.

Some Successful Arrangements

Some plate arrangements seem generally successful in pleasing customers. Without considering them as prescriptive or all-inclusive, the restaurateur might experiment with them.

High-backed salad or appetizer A leaf of lettuce is especially high at the back of the plate; in the very front toward the diner is the main element—crab meat chunks for example. The entire composition is triangular with the lettuce leaf as the base of the triangle and the crab meat apex squarely in front of the diner. Garnishes bracket the mound of crab meat or, more precisely, the avalanche of crab meat.

Oval arrangement of a long item On an oval dish with a broad side facing the diner or on a round plate, a long food item, a trout, for example, is placed diagonally from the high right side to the low left side. The vegetable is tucked in the right side; a small garnish is placed in the left side above the element.

Basic triangular arrangement The main item is placed on the right side of the plate, the larger (in surface area) vegetable in the left lower quarter, the smaller vegetable or garnish above it. High items should be behind low items regardless of how much surface area they cover. This arrangement is mistakenly avoided by many cooks who place the vegetable items flanking the main dish.

Complete meal formal arrangement If the plate were marked with numerals like a clock, the 6 would be directly in front of the guest. The meat is best placed across the numerals 4 through 7, any garnish or separate sauce at the 3, the potatoes at 1 and 2, and the vegetable at 8, 9, and 10.

Accessories

The eye appeal of food can be improved by the use of proper serviceware without significantly altering the food. For many operations this may be the best approach, because almost no labor is involved. The restaurateur buys his visual appeal in the form of attractive specialty serviceware, disposable accessories, and decorative treatments.

Despite successful accessorization, the basic problem—the appearance of the food—still remains. Since some customers cannot be directed away from the appearance of the food itself, accessorization as the only means of increasing a food's eye appeal might best be limited to those items that simply need jazzing up, a touch of glamor, and not a complete program of decoration.

Specialty Serviceware

Specialty dishes, glasses, and cooking/serving utensils dramatize a food item. They place it in a setting that maximizes its virtues and minimizes its weaknesses. For example, a beef stew on an 11-inch dinner plate does not look appetizing. The same stew in an individual casserole, possibly a miniature earthenware cauldron, has tremendous appeal. The package has vastly improved the appearance of the product.

Even foods that are basically appealing are improved by the right packaging. Any food looks more elegant on silver service. Any bread looks better in a white napkin. Any salad looks better in a wooden bowl. Any drink looks better in a crystal glass.

The crystal and silver specialty dish may suggest elegance. Copper vessels lined with stainless steel or tin, earthenware in natural tones, or sizzler platters can imply that the dish is made to order. Wooden salad bowls, iced fruit supremes, or iron skillets can represent a quality standard of preparation. Chafing dishes, soufflé cups, or oven casseroles can also lend the food the appearance of being a high cost item (when it is not) because the serviceware is expensive or is used for expensive items.

Any of this appeal is available to the operator who is willing to invest what can be a substantial sum. In addition, a restaurateur considering wholesale adoption of this approach might well consider the inevitable chaos in the dishroom when ten different items, some of which cannot be stacked or racked, are dumped. Table 3.1 offers some suggestions for the use of specialty serviceware that adds visual appeal to dishes.

Table 3.1 Specialty Serviceware for Eye Appeal

Item	Description	Use
Artichoke plate	Usually a white porcelain plate with a central cup surrounded by leaflike compartments	Hors d'oeuvres salads, chips and dips, nuts
Au gratin dish	Rounds and ovals of all dimensions and capacities in different colors and two-tone combinations	Any liquid food, any dish made from oddments, anything that can be covered with cheese or bread crumbs

Table 3.1 Specialty Serviceware for Eye Appeal (cont)

Item	Description	Use
Baking dish	Colorful portion-size dish of enamel on iron or porcelain	Sizzler platters, individual portions of baked items, vegetables too messy to portion
Baskets	All shapes, colors, weaves, and sizes available	Any baked goods; lined-with-glass dishes for hot foods, with napkins for fried foods
Beer glasses	Schooner, pilsner glasses, mugs	For salads, desserts, appetizer cocktails
Brandy snifter	Different sizes and qualities	Fruit salads, cold soups, seafood cocktails, desserts
Copperware	Saucepans, pots and pans, baking dishes, au gratins with and without covers; generally copper on the outside, tin or stainless steel on the inside	Stews, braised dishes, vegetables, any dish that does not look attractive spread on a plate or cut into pieces
Crocks	Miniature pickle crocks of gray and two-tone brown	Salad dressings, relishes, stews

Table 3.1 Specialty Serviceware for Eye Appeal (cont)

Item	Description	Use
Crystal	Glassware, serving dishes, specialty items	Any cold foods
Glass bells	Glass covers with a little knob on top	"Under glass" treatment of anything, including hamburgers
Ironware	Pots, skillets in all sizes	Service of vegetables, stews, casserole items, pot roasts
Oaken buckets	Small replicas of well buckets	Soups, salads, relishes, mixed fried foods, chicken dishes
Planks	Hard wooden planks about 8 by 16 inches, rectangular or oval	Fish and other foods that break up easily in handling
Pots de crème	Elegant little porcelain cups with covers	Egg dishes, mushy desserts, soft vegetables
Shells	Real or earthenware scallop shells	Fish dish au gratin, seafood cocktails, deep-fried broken shrimp
Stoneware	Wide variety of small vessels including onion soup crocks	Stews, vegetables, soups, desserts that spread on the plate

Disposable Accessorization

Opportunities to use disposable accessorization have increased considerably since the time when chefs made "pants" (frou-frous) for lamb chops from butcher's paper.

Many paper, plastic, and wood decorations are available, and most can be used in fairly good taste in at least some food operations. Although the more expensive operation may be limited to frou-frous of gold foil, paper lace doilies, and perhaps frill toothpicks, the fast food operation and the informal restaurant can offer their customers the fun of inexpensive disposable novelties that at least add visual appeal and may also entertain.

> Toothpicks with American flags, Uncle Sam and other cartoon heads, frills, emblems, and animal forms
>
> Portion control cups of plastic and decorated paper, filled with colorful convenience elements
>
> Disposable serviceware—from a soup bowl to a coffee cup—available in a wide variety of patterns and designs in paper and plastic
>
> Paper goods such as napkins, doilies, place mats, and wrappings (for baked potatoes) in a wide variety of attractive designs or even custom designs
>
> Novelty decorations such as pinwheels, Japanese parasols, paper clowns, and so on

Decorative Treatments

The restaurateur can improve food's visual appeal with some decorative showmanship to impress the customer. Fire and ice are standard in many quality operations that flambé* foods or serve seafood cock-

* See *Showmanship in the Dining Room,* in this series.

tails and fresh fruits embedded in crushed ice (or in special dishes with inserts resting in ice).

Any operation can cash in on the appeal of fire: Without even flambéing foods with liqueurs, the excitement of fire can be exploited by planting sparklers in food items. Candles slightly thicker than a toothpick can be floated on croutons in soup.

Crushed ice is impressive no matter how it is used, and it is readily available to everyone. In many instances it can be recovered in the dishroom and used again. Juice glasses can be embedded in ice, cocktails served in pre-iced glasses, and seafood cocktails, melons, and mollusks can be made more visually stimulating with the addition of ice.

Fresh flowers can often perk up foods visually. Some are edible, after being thoroughly washed to remove sprays, and can be used in salads: daisies, roses, marigolds, carnations, orchids, orange blossoms, honeysuckle, chrysanthemums, gladiolas, pansies, violets, peonies, and tulips. Or they can even be used as vessels for foods. Many customers would enjoy the visual appeal of a bright red tulip stuffed with chicken salad. Even scattering blooms on a plate, whether the customer eats them or not, has a strong visual impact. A tropical cocktail, for example, can be highlighted with a small orchid blossom perched on the edge of the glass.

As another serving idea, some operations might find that sizzler platters make steaks, chops, or roasted fowl much more appealing to the eye. Or, items presented on a bed of rock salt in a black iron baking pan—stuffed oysters or clams, for example—have a similar strong appeal. In addition, attractively arranged skewers give broiled meats extra appeal. Or, to offer still more excitement, try flaming swords.

Eye Appeal for Quantity Food Presentation

The problems of making a cafeteria line attractive would not be unfamiliar to the chefs of the nineteenth century who created "classical" food decoration for fish, hams, fowl, cold sauce dishes (chaudfroid), and so on. Their clients, like guests in a cafeteria or in a dining room offering food "bars," selected their food from massed displays of the entire meal. The problems are essentially the same: The food must look attractive to "sell," the attractiveness must last throughout the service period, and each food item must remain appetizing as portions are taken from it.

Unfortunately, attempting to solve the problem in a classical manner, using very careful decoration and quantities of aspic, would make the solution part of the problem. The labor for classical decoration is not available; the declining standards of the culinary art salons at hotel and restaurant shows give ample evidence of the fact. If it were available, however, the cost of properly dismantling the buffet items so that they maintained their appeal during service would be prohibitive: At some nineteenth-century banquets at least two waiters and a carver were necessary for each diner.

Modern eye-appealing presentations must be consistent with the realities of present-day restaurant operations. Eye appeal can be given displays of food in the dining room and cafeteria lines so that the food sells, looks good throughout the meal period, and is attractively portioned with the skills available to most operations, and at minimal—if any—extra cost.

Dining Room Displays

Many restaurateurs have discovered that bringing food in quantity into the dining room helps merchandise the operation, and, more importantly perhaps, it cuts down on costs. Unlimited salad bars, for example, seem to be a bonus that offers a great value for the money to the customer, and they eliminate the high cost of maintaining a stock of varied salad elements and the wages of a pantry man. The rolling cart service of hors d'oeuvres, main dishes, soups, and desserts offers at least the benefit of reduced costs and some merchandising value, if not "value for the money" appeal.

If the food on these displays is not eye appealing, however, both the operational and merchandising advantages are lost. In addition, since the display is in the dining room, the operator has an obligation to make it attractive and keep it attractive as part of the decor.

Food Displays

Frills and fanciness are not necessary for eye appeal in a dining room food display. The local "Steak and 'Something'" with a salad bar and a flea-market decor cannot use a formal ice carving without seeming a little ridiculous. Rather, the unpretentious restaurant can rely on the eye appeal of the food itself when it is massed into a large, effective display. For example, the restaurateur can open 20 one-gallon jugs of different pickles and pour them into clear bowls for a startling, eye appealing display. There is color interest, texture interest, and yet a pleasing modernistic simplicity. Some original accessorization enhances the effect without overwhelming the food. Instead of ordinary glass bowls, for example, giant snifters, fish bowls, apothecary jars, or old-fashioned candy jars might be used. Without decorating the food itself, the restaurateur can add appealing details.

In developing ways to enhance dining room displays, the restaurateur might consider these guidelines:

1. *Make it big.* It is best to choose items that will not deteriorate, either because of their natural preservation (pickles, for example) or because they are in a refrigerated or iced display, so that an ample quantity can be put out at once.

2. *Buy consumer accessorization.* Gourmet stores, antique shops, and quality department stores have truly exciting articles for the display of food: earthenware crocks, jugs, glass pitchers, wooden bowls, ironware, tin-lined copper, even modern plastic. These kinds of items cannot be offered by institutional manufacturers because of their limited market.

3. *Build in the display.* If possible, the display table or area should seem to be built into the facility. For example, a rotating 12-foot-wide lazy Susan that is half in the dining room and half in the kitchen is impressive visually no matter what is put on it. Similarly, dishes that fit into a table look much more impressive than dishes that sit on a table.

4. *Use ice.* Ice is an excellent accessory because the guest cannot have the same quantity or variety of ice in his own home. It makes every cold food look better, and in many instances it can actually hide a weak appearance.

5. *Use light, but not colored lights.* The food should be colorful and the colors of the food should be

used dramatically. The whole display area should be well lit, but with soft white lighting or spotlighting that does not distort the food's natural color.

Ideas for Eye Appealing Displays

1 Wine carafes filled with juices, each with a silver neck label and standing in champagne buckets filled with ice; have at least ten juices
2 A tremendous mound of cooked shrimp in the shell with the heads on, and seaweed on ice in a rowboat made of rough-hewn "driftwood"
3 Mini bushel baskets lined with checked vinyl, "spilling out" cooked vegetables to garnish salad greens
4 At least three dozen pickles and pickled salads (all available preprepared) in mini pickle barrels
5 A "push cart" filled with fresh fruit

Rolling Carts

Rolling carts for hors d'oeuvres, main dishes, and desserts have an obvious operational benefit. At the very least, the waiter does not have to return to the kitchen to serve these items. If enough items are sold from the cart, there is no need for anyone to prepare desserts, for example, and so at least one less kitchen worker is needed.

In addition, the rolling cart has a virtually unique benefit: It allows the restaurateur to sell items he could not otherwise sell because of their appearance. It adds immeasurable visual appeal to items with weak appearance. When the waiter rolls the cart to the table, he presents the dish—for example, a large game pie or a whole braised bass. Even if part of the dish has already been served, it can still look attractive in the cart. Then the waiter serves the patron. The individual portion may not look particularly appetizing, but the diner has the visual impression of the entire pie or fish and eats his meal with relish. The same portion, because of its appearance, could not be served from the kitchen: it would look like a leftover.

Bouillabaisse or any other soup or stew made of a variety of odd-shaped ingredients is a fantastic item served from a giant copper cauldron. Served in a bowl from the kitchen, it loses its appeal; the customer can't identify the lumps on his plate.

Eye Appeal in Cafeteria Service

Restaurateurs and institutional feeders with cafeteria operations can surely borrow from the techniques that increase eye appeal in dining rooom display and buffets. For example, nothing prevents the cafeteria operator from using an ice piece made from a mold if its carving by a worker is impossible. Theme decoration and quality accessorization can lighten the impersonality and monotony of stainless steel or plastic-covered equipment. The cafeteria display area as a whole and the steamtable, salad, dessert, bread, and beverage counters have their own imperatives for presentation and service that increase the visual appeal of the food.

Cafeteria Display Area as a Whole

The Importance of Cleanliness Food loses its attractiveness if it is displayed in a dirty facility. Disregarding for a moment the most important consideration in maintaining a clean cafeteria service line—the health of the customer—it is vitally important that any area the customer can see be absolutely immaculate. It must also be kept neat during the service. A program of cafeteria sanitation would include the following high-priority procedures:

1 Lime incrustations on steamtables made by hard water should be removed periodically (as needed) with special descaling agents.

2 After every meal period, the top of the steamtable and racks should be washed, rinsed, and polished.
3 Metal and glass shelves of display racks should be washed, dried, and polished. Special attention must be paid to bolts, screws, hinges, and braces where dirt accumulates.
4 The outside of the counter has to be cleaned after every meal period with a special cleaner for the material of which it is made: stainless steel, vinyl, leather, and so on.
5 Visible equipment must be cleaned and polished.
6 The floor area behind the counter has to be immaculate. Wooden duck boards, for example, have to be bleached white.

Employee Responsibility for Cleanliness During the service, employees should be trained to maintain the appearance of the counter properly and to serve neatly or at least clean up after themselves immediately. Three problems are especially common: (1) food fragments and gravy are dropped from the rim of plates onto the counter; (2) pans are neither replaced, consolidated, nor scraped down, and the food on display sits in the middle of an incrustation that seems a week old; (3) rags are left on the counter.

Maintaining Food's Natural Eye Appeal

Most food is itself attractive without embellishment. Many cafeterias allow it to deteriorate during the service, so that midway through the meal much of its appeal is lost. For example, butter chips are pleasant looking, if not exactly eye arresting. When they melt in their little paper or foil trays, however, they become unpleasant. Beef stew is no great visual treat, but beef stew with a layer of congealed gravy on top is in bad shape. Among other examples of unnecessary visual deterioration, those listed (with solutions) in Table 4.1 seem to be very common.

34 ADDING EYE APPEAL TO FOODS

Table 4.1 Common Problems of Visual Deterioration on Cafeteria Lines with Suggested Solutions

Problem	Solution
Vegetable fatigue in the steam table	Use half- or third-sized pans instead of full pans.
Congealed gravy	Avoid flour thickening; stir pans carefully; dot surfaces with butter.
Clotted creamers	Use portion packs or closed creamers.
Green eggs	Use small quantities in cooking; avoid contact with metal utensils.
Scrambled meatloaf, lasagna, etc.	Preportion on shallow pans.
Wilted greens	Use iced display areas if refrigeration cannot be used.
Mushy fried foods	Use perforated pans for holding.
Gray meats	Dry hold with infrared heating elements instead of steam holding.
Meats in grease	Hold on racks instead of on flat pans, or use perforated pans in flat pans.
Soggy pasta	Hold sauce and pasta separately so that pasta does not continue to cook or soak up sauce.
Melted butter	Use a chip dispenser with refrigeration by ice or electricity.
Discolored dressings	Use pump or pressure dispenser.

Table 4.1 Common Problems of Visual Deterioration on Cafeteria Lines with Suggested Solutions (cont)

Problem	Solution
Melted chiffon pies	These and other gelatin-based desserts must be in a refrigerated case, not just refrigerated from the bottom.

Overall Eye Appeal

Since a cafeteria counter is a display of merchandise, the cafeteria operator can learn from professional supermarket displays and department store windows. Both manage to display large quantities of merchandise, of various sorts, in some organized manner and still preserve the individual identity of each item. They also have techniques for reducing visual monotony and stimulating customer interest.

Supermarkets and department stores use outstanding accessorization even when the merchandise is fairly dull. The same techniques applied to a cafeteria could be the use of bright red enamel pots instead of stainless steel inserts, checkered napkins in wicker baskets for crackers, flowers and ferns on the counter, or an autumnal display of gourds, pumpkins, and leaves right in the middle of the line.

Display designers use height effectively, too. Similarly, the cafeteria operator can use pedestals, cake stands, and footed dishes, so that individual items on the line are highlighted and the whole line is varied.

The operator might also try to solve a problem unique to food merchandising by choosing menu items that can be displayed, held, and served attractively from a cafeteria line. If the operation cannot handle lasagna so that it looks appetizing all the time—perhaps by putting it in individual casseroles—it should probably be left out of the menu cycle. If broccoli spears die in the steam table with depressing regularity, maybe chopped broccoli or none at all is the reasonable alternative.

Once the menu is determined, the operator or someone considering overall appearance should specify the pan or dish in which each menu item will be displayed. It is unattractive, destructive, and unnecessary to fish sweet potatoes from a deep-well pan, for example, and it looks unappetizing to keep stewed tomatoes in a shallow pan.

A sense of order is the final requisite for a good overall design. Of course, rows must be neat, but some consideration should be given to: (1) the color and form of the items that are placed next to each other; (2) the placement of service utensils and condiments on the counter; (3) the logic of the customer's self-service; and (4) the maximization of the server's efforts to make everything look appealing.

Steam Table Eye Appeal

If the operator considers the appearance of foods in steam table pans from the other side of the counter, he will notice five recurring defects that, once corrected, will make the food much more attractive:

1 Pans appear almost empty most of the time because full-sized pans are used instead of half-, third-, quarter-, or even one sixth-sized pans. Every customer after about the third has the impression that the choicest pieces have already been dished out.
2 Portions are not separated. For example, instead of being able to pick up three slices of pot roast nicely shingled in a separate pile with a perforated spatula, the server is obliged to fish the slices from the gravy with a fork and maneuver the dripping pieces to the plate. Anything in slices should be

overlapped in parallel rows; rounded items should be lined up evenly, and so on. Service should be from back to front.

3   The steam table pans are not garnished. In most instances some element of the food can be used as a garnish. For example, cheese strips can be crisscrossed over macaroni and cheese and browned. Or a garnish can be added. Besides the standard but acceptable greens, the operator can use more creative garnishes: beef stew, for example, can be decorated with a latticework of biscuit dough or with individual dumplings.

4   The pans have not been arranged with any consideration of the color and texture of neighboring pans.

5   Everything is flat. When possible, items should be displayed in pans so that they appear three-dimensional. Corned beef slices can be draped over cabbage quarters, turkey can be placed over stuffing, sausages on apple fritters, and so on.

The operator might also use individual casseroles for many items instead of portioning them from the steam table pan. Foods like chili, garnished with alternate rows of finely chopped green pepper and onions, can look good in the steam table pan, and acceptable in a bowl, but they seem unappetizing on a flat plate. A casserole presentation, with the chili in a ring of white rice or macaroni, solves the problem.

Salad Counter Eye Appeal

Assuming that salad plates themselves are attractive (see Chapter 6), arranging them well is a matter of neatness, color balance, and an appreciation of the customer's angle of vision.

It is axiomatic that salad plates must be arranged in orderly rows. Rows of similar items might best be placed on parallel diagonals instead of at right angles to the sides of the counter. The elements of each salad must be on the same side of the salad and oriented the same way. For example, if a salad has a pear half on one side, all such salads should be arranged with the pears on the same side and with all the points facing one way—ideally, up and slightly to the side.

Color balance between the groups of salads is important if their individual features are to be highlighted. Macaroni salad next to potato salad looks like potato salad; macaroni salad next to stuffed prunes looks like macaroni salad. The objective is to have the display resemble a bouquet of salads.

The customer's angle of vision is an important consideration. Ideally, salads will be set in a gently sloping mound of crushed ice so that the customer looks down on them without leaning over the counter. Basically, the position of the salad should follow the slope of the counter: The highest point of each plate should be farthest from the customer.

Dessert Counter Eye Appeal

Some of the observations made about salads apply equally well to desserts. Certainly the rows must be even, color should be balanced, and items should be oriented similarly. All the points of pieces of pie, for example, should face the same way.

Desserts offer a tremendous opportunity for using dramatic serviceware. Instead of placing desserts in cereal bowls, cake plates, and monkey (nappy) dishes, they can be individually accented and enhanced by using glassware, footed dishes, ice cream fountain dishes, or small porcelain or stoneware pots. Variety in service gives the impression that each dessert has been individually prepared even though the customer is probably aware that most desserts are convenience products and have not been just prepared in the kitchen.

5

Eye Appeal for Buffets

Buffet service offers the restaurateur several operational benefits. With proper planning, kitchen and dining room personnel can be reduced on a day when the buffet is offered: Many seven-day operations give most of their help their holiday that day. Other restaurateurs find it a convenient way to accommodate parties in private rooms without additional service or production personnel. Still others emulate private clubs and American plan hotels and use the buffet as a novel event to promote the establishment and stimulate customer interest.

In any buffet, the customer serves himself at least part of the meal. He is often compensated for his effort by the value for the money appeal of unlimited portions and a wide choice of menu items. On the other hand, the restaurateur defends his profits by making sure that the buffet includes items that are inexpensive but so visually appealing that the customer wants to eat them, perhaps in preference to the roasts, whole fowl, and hams that also appear on the buffet. The buffet is made especially attractive to please the patron but also to protect the profit.

In planning a buffet that includes the entire meal, the operator should consider five factors that contribute to its visual appeal:

1. Arrangement of the buffet in the room
2. Nonedible decoration

3 Major edible pieces
4 Decorated platters
5 Arrangement of the buffet items themselves

Arrangement of the Buffet in the Room

In commercial operations, the buffet is set at one side of the room and tables are set at the other, with an ample aisle for passage between. The main buffet line can take numerous forms using combinations of oblong, round, half-round, quarter-round, trapezoid, and curved tables (see Figure 5.1).

When the buffet is to be very elaborate, most experienced restaurateurs set up several buffet units in the room instead of having one continuous line. As most decorative effects are more suited to cold items, the main line has the most involved visual effects. One, two, or three smaller lines are used for hot foods, desserts, salads, or beverages or for several courses in combination.

The main buffet's visual impact usually rests with the effective presentation of food. The smaller buffets can be decorated attractively. For example, a dessert buffet may be a stylized old-fashioned ice cream fountain; a hot-food line can look like a copper kitchen.

Whenever possible the main buffet line should be positioned so that diners can appreciate its attractiveness as they enter the room or rise from their tables.

Operational factors should also be considered, including the flow of the customers to, from, and along the buffet and the flow of the personnel attending the buffet to and from the kitchen. Buffets in the center of the room and buffets of angled tables speed the service, but they also prevent access to the kitchen except by passing through the customers, and they necessitate decorating from all angles.

Figure 5.1 Tables of varying shapes may be used in combination to form the main buffet line.

Nonedible Decoration

There are two major types of nonedible decoration for buffets: (1) decorative items that are actually room furnishings, accessories, or scenic effects, and (2) decorative elements that supposedly belong to culinary art, such as ice carvings, tallow work, wax sculpture, and spun-sugar work.

Today in the United States, it is easier to buy, make, or rent props and decorations than it is to find a chef who can prepare attractive, tasteful culinary "art." It is almost too much to ask that an individual be a good cook and a competent sculptor.

Decorating Buffets with Accessories and Props

Many modern buffets are designed with a definite theme, limited only by the imagination and resources of the designer. He creates a stage set on which food is eaten. For example, he may decide to create a German Brauhaus complete with oak tables, beer steins, waiters in lederhosen, and a buffet table loaded with sausages, pork, hams, and German specialties. Or, he could choose a pirate theme and drape the entire room and buffet tables with nets and sails, buoys, anchors, ships' wheels, and so on.

Certain themes enjoy a continuing popularity:

1 *Roaring twenties* Featuring old cars in the dining room and sometimes "bathtub gin" punch in a bathtub, flapper or gangster costumes on service personnel, and so on
2 *Harvest time* Plenty of barn wood, pumpkins, sheaves of wheat, bales of hay, and wagon wheels
3 *Wild West* Split-rail fencing, chuck wagons, saddles and bridles, cowboy clothes
4 *Hawaiian* Leis, other flowers, roasting pigs, grass skirts, and beach sand

5 *Italian* Red and white checked tablecloths, candles in wine bottles, moustached waiters in long white aprons

The classic formal buffet relies on white linen, crystal, silver, and flowers as the dominant decor notes. Obvious decorative themes lend themselves to holiday buffets.

Culinary "Art" Decorations: Ice Carving

Unlike tallow carvings or butter molds, which require great skill, ice carvings can be done by anyone, because a vague approximation of the form of the figure suffices. An ice cornucopia for fruit or a boat shape for shrimp is hardly as difficult to sculpt as a sugar United Nations or a life-size butter American eagle.

Tools for ice carving Most ice carvings are made from a block of manufactured ice about 20 inches wide and 44 inches high. The more experienced carver can do a simple design in a cool area without refrigeration; slower workers must work either in the ice house where the ice was purchased or in a walk-in refrigerator.

Tools for ice carving are simple, inexpensive, and available in hardware stores anywhere:

> Ice hooks or tongs for moving the carving
> Shovel for cleaning the work area
> Rubber gloves for handling the ice and protecting the hands during carving
> Whisk broom for cleaning the carving while working
> Puncture type can opener for making outlines on the block of ice
> Ice pick for making outlines on the block

Three-cornered wood chisel for marking and grooving

Small woodworking chisels, from ¼ to 2 inches wide, for general carving

Short-handled and long-handled ice shavers (also called ice chippers; six steel points in a malleable iron body with a wooden handle) for removing large areas of ice

Rasp for making round edges

Cross-cut saw for cutting away large pieces of ice

In addition, a metal cutting torch, an electric saw, and shaped chisels can be used to advantage if they are available.

Handling the ice Manufactured ice is not particularly fragile. If it is moved carefully on a wooden carrier (like a sled) it seldom breaks or cracks. As an added precaution, most carvers allow it to rest outside the freezer for 30 to 40 minutes before carving so that it is not brittle. Any cracks that do occur in handling can usually be repaired by holding the pieces together and returning the carving to the freezer, or cementing them with slush (or slush and table salt) and refreezing. Once the ice is carved, a piece of cloth under it will prevent it from sliding around on the floor or work table.

Subjects for ice carvings As a carving medium, ice is best suited to subjects recognizable by their outlines, not by their surface detail. Unless the carver is really expert, blocky silhouettes are better than subjects that require the carver to create thin ice supports in airy space. The most common subjects have both these qualities: a swan, a cornucopia, a shrimp boat, a fish, a basket, or a candle holder and candle stick, among others.

Although the carving is three dimensional, it is actually carved as a two-dimensional figure. Only a token effort is made to create a carving that can be viewed from other angles than straight on. In essence, this explains the success of nonartists in the medium: They do not have to worry about perspective.

Once a subject is chosen, it is outlined or traced on a piece of graph paper. Then, using the graph paper square as a scale, it is patiently enlarged to the exact size of the carving, usually 20 by 40 inches. The new, enlarged-to-size outline becomes a pattern or template for the carving once it is cut out of the drawing paper.

Making the carving Once the template is made, the rest of the carving is very simple. An experienced carver can make a simple standard carving in 30 to 40 minutes.

1 Place the template against the block of ice.
2 Use a can opener or ice pick to trace the outline of the template onto the ice. If necessary, use a three-cornered chisel to deepen the outline; it must last or be renewed during the entire time of carving.
3 Remove the template, which can be reused.
4 Use a saw first to remove large pieces of excess ice. Make a second series of cuts with the saw at the places from which ice will be removed by chiseling or scraping. These stop cuts, or relief cuts, are extremely important because they prevent breakage and excess removal of ice later on. They need not go through the piece but should be deep enough to be definite.
5 The scrapers are used next to outline the figure roughly. They remove significant amounts of ice, but not so much as the saw and with less precision than the chisel and rasp.

6 Use the whisk broom to keep the working area clear of chips. Use the shovel to keep the floor or work bench clean.
7 Use the chisel to finish forming the detail of the silhouette. The finest work must be done last and quickly with the chisel, ice pick, or rasp. Otherwise, it will melt away before the carving is completed. Do not overcarve.
8 The pronged scrapers can be used to rough up the surface of the ice so that the piece seems to have texture and is not so transparent that it cannot be clearly seen.
9 The carving completes itself by melting slightly on display (30 minutes) so that it sparkles when seen. It should *not* be washed.

Display of carvings For display, the carving is usually placed in a metal pan or waterproof box about 8 inches larger than the carving and 4 or 5 inches deep. Most carvings will last 5 or 6 hours without difficulty, but fragile carvings melt faster than blocky ones.

The bottom of the pan can be filled with flowers, leaves, ferns, seaweed, or colored pebbles, depending on the carving. Often ice carvings are lighted with colored spotlights from behind and from inside the box.

Major Pieces

Decorated large food items such as whole hams, turkeys, and fish are frequently used to make buffets more appealing. Although they could be prepared to be eaten themselves, most often they serve only as decorations or center pieces. They lend eye appeal to the buffet as a whole and to platters of sliced or prepared food such as ham, turkey, or salmon salad.

There are four major steps in the preparation of these items:

1. Preparation of the item itself
2. Preparation of the coating for the item
3. Preparation of the decorative elements
4. Assembling the piece

Preparation of the Item

If the item will be eaten, which is rarely the case, it must be fully cleaned, prepared, and cooked by some appropriate method: roasting, poaching, and so on.

For most buffets, the major pieces do not have to be so carefully prepared because they are simply decorations. Sometimes raw hams and turkeys are decorated. In fact, many cooks decorate mock food made of mashed potatoes or cooked ground meat because there is no need to expose a fairly expensive piece of meat to room temperatures, which makes it unsafe to eat, when it will not be used at the time.

In either case, the article has to be trimmed and formed so that it is easy to coat. Hams sometimes have to be filled in. Turkeys may be trussed so that they are attractive on the platter. The fins and tails of whole fish have to be trimmed so that they look like stylized fins and tails.

Preparation of the Coating

Two coating sauces are needed: chaudfroid and aspic. Both gel when cold; they differ in that chaudfroid is opaque and either white or colored, and aspic is usually colorless but always clear. Again, if the food is to be eaten, these sauces must be well-flavored and properly prepared according to recipes that may be found in any major professional cookbook. On the other hand, following the general practice, they, too, are often imitative.

Chaudfroid is made by preparing unflavored gelatin according to the instructions on the package but doubling the proportions of gelatin to liquid (about 2 ounces per quart instead of 1 ounce) so that a tough, durable gel is formed. Colors are made by combining the gelatin mixture with either white sauce or mayonnaise, counting these as part of the original liquid, and then adding colored food purees or food coloring.

> Gelatin plus mayonnaise or white sauce yields white chaudfroid.
>
> White chaudfroid plus pureed pimiento yields red chaudfroid.
>
> White chaudfroid plus pureed spinach yields green chaudfroid.
>
> White chaudfroid plus hard egg yolk yields yellow chaudfroid.
>
> White chaudfroid plus brown sauce yields brown chaudfroid.
>
> Aspic is simply the gelatin and the water with or without food colorings.

The coatings should be prepared carefully, strained, and then allowed to sit at room temperature so that air bubbles can escape. Then they can be slowly cooled until almost thick. The more slowly they are cooled—in a refrigerator as opposed to over ice—the more durable the final gel will be.

Preparation of the Decorative Elements

Three kinds of decorations are commonly used for major pieces:

1 *Aspic or chaudfroid cutouts.* First the coating mixtures are poured in a thin layer in a slightly oiled

plate and then chilled. When they are gelled, truffle or aspic cutters (which resemble tiny cookie cutters) can be used to stamp out plain geometric figures such as squares, circles, hexagons, or parallelograms, or decorations such as stars, hex signs, flowers, or leaves. As the decorations are made, they are lifted from the tray with a toothpick and placed in a cup of cold water for storage until use.

2 *Cutouts from natural foods.* Thin pieces of carrot, truffle, tomato peel, cucumber peel, orange skin, lemon peel, and so on can be cut freehand or with truffle cutters into decorative shapes.

3 *Real food.* Any attractive, neat food can be used: notched cucumber slices, half prunes, half cherries, sliced canned peaches, pickle fans, thin slices of citrus fruits, sliced radishes, hard-cooked egg slices, pimiento strips, black or green olive halves or slices, sliced mushrooms, and so on.

Assembling the Major Piece

1 Making a design is the first step in assembling and decorating the piece. The cook takes a piece of paper the size of the food item and sketches a design on it. The design should be simple, tasteful, and pleasant, but it must be neat: good choices are a hex sign, a mosaic, a simple geometric arrangement, or a floral pattern.

2 As the design is being made, the food item should be completely cooled in the refrigerator on a wire rack.

3 Chaudfroid and aspic in appropriate colors should be made.

4 The decorations should be made.

5 When the piece has cooled *completely*, remove it from the refrigerator on the wire rack over a sheet pan. Spoon the chaudfroid sauce over the article.

Try to spoon it evenly so that "drippings" do not mar the evenness of the surface.

6 Return the article to the refrigerator so that the sauce gels *completely*.

7 Repeat steps 5 and 6 as many times as needed to coat the article with a very smooth glaze. Then let it stay in the refrigerator for 1 hour.

8 Remove the article from the refrigerator, and, following the pattern, apply the decorations.

   a When possible, insert the decoration in the chaudfroid by cutting a place for it. When the decoration has been cut out with an aspic cutter, the same cutter can be used to remove a bit of the chaudfroid to make room. This procedure gives the article an inlaid, integrated appearance.

   b Holding the decoration on the point of a toothpick, dip it in aspic before applying it so that it sticks to the chaudfroid.

9 When the decoration has been applied, chill the item again.

10 After 1 hour, remove it from the refrigerator and coat it with clear aspic. To achieve a smooth glaze, several coats separated by intervals of refrigeration may be necessary.

Some Decoration Schemes

Simple truffle or black olive cutouts on white chaudfroid—for example, stars, half moons, or dots.

A single large flower of an egg-yolk slice with pimiento petals, chive stem, and leek-leaf leaves.

A checkerboard of red-and-green aspic squares or parallelograms.

A fringe of "holly" with half cranberries and leek-leaf leaves.

A central design of peach slices fanned around a maraschino cherry.

Platter Decoration

Most buffet dishes consist of attractive platters of fairly ordinary items: marinated vegetables, sliced cold meats, chunks of fowl, hors d'oeuvre salads, green salads, preserved fish, and so on. Of course, these items themselves can be attractive, and the following chapters are devoted to enhancing their appearance. But the buffet offers opportunities that individual plates do not. For example, a customer's plate cannot be entirely surrounded by crab apples set in pineapple rings, although a single crab apple and a single ring might be used to garnish a cold corned beef plate. A large platter of corned beef that contains half of a corned beef intact with overlapping slices in front of it can give a very good effect.

The platter can also be decorated with a single dramatic item that would simply be too large or too expensive for the customer's own plate. A pineapple basket filled with preserved sweet and sour fruits (*aceto-dolce*) can be a very attractive garnish for a platter of cold meat, but not for a plate.

Platter Border Decorations

Anything that can be used on an individual plate may be used to border a platter, and the most attractive decorations are usually made of small items surrounding a main item. Neatness and color balance (no more than three colors) are important as well as the size of the decoration and the size of the platter border and contents.

Although it is not necessary, it is wise to dip the decorations for platters in clear aspic so that they stick to the platter and retain a fresh-looking gloss.

52 ADDING EYE APPEAL TO FOODS

The items marked with an asterisk are discussed in greater detail below and in Chapter 7, along with other garnishes and decorations to which this approach can be adapted.

1. Hard-cooked egg slices topped with cutouts of truffle, black olive, or pimiento
2. Wedges of hard-cooked egg and chickory
3. Lemon slices that have been notched with a channel cutter
4. Wedges of orange peel filled with colored gelatin*
5. Mushroom caps*
6. Carrot curls and cucumber twists*
7. Pickle fans*
8. Stuffed olives
9. Cutouts, as suggested above for the decoration of major pieces, on evenly cut pieces of vegetable or meat
10. Cutouts of cold meat—for example, alternating diamonds of ham and sliced white-meat turkey, shingled around the platter
11. Cubes of gelled aspic
12. Flowers of half a cherry tomato in a clump of curly parsley
13. Vegetable flowers*
14. Small hollowed half tomatoes filled with vegetables*
15. Peas arranged in grapelike clusters on a celery leaf

Feature Decorations for Platters

Platters are given eye appeal by placing a decorative item at one end of the platter and then arranging the food with this decoration as an anchor point. For example, a single squab chicken can be decorated with chaudfroid and placed at one end of an oval platter filled with neatly arranged chicken parts. Or a gelatin mold, called a timbale, can be placed in the center of a round platter surrounded by rolls of meat or vegetable salad.

There are three general categories of large platter decorations:

1 Vegetable flowers or figures
2 Timbales
3 Fruit decorations

Vegetable flowers and figures Vegetable flowers and figures present two problems: (1) Most are inedible, which is why they are not used on individual plates; (2) unless they are done well, they are absolutely tasteless, merely crude examples of the decorative effects associated in many peoples' minds with the worst type of cheap catering.

They might be rated on the basis of how many pounds of vegetables it takes before the cook can make an acceptable product. Radish roses can be learned with 1 pound of practice; a swan from a potato or an alligator from a carrot might require a ton of vegetables. Some might be attempted with available personnel to see how practical they are for the particular operation.

Onion water lily Starting at the stem end of a medium-sized, unpeeled Spanish onion, cut eight equal sections to the root end (without cutting through it) to form the petals of the flower. Place the onion in boiling water, remove from heat, and allow to stand for 5 minutes. Put the onion in a pan of cold water and allow it to cool. Using a paring knife, carefully separate each layer of onion to make the petals. Place celery leaves under the "lily" to make the pad.

Beet or turnip rose Peel the vegetable and trim it so that it is completely round. Cut a thin slice from one

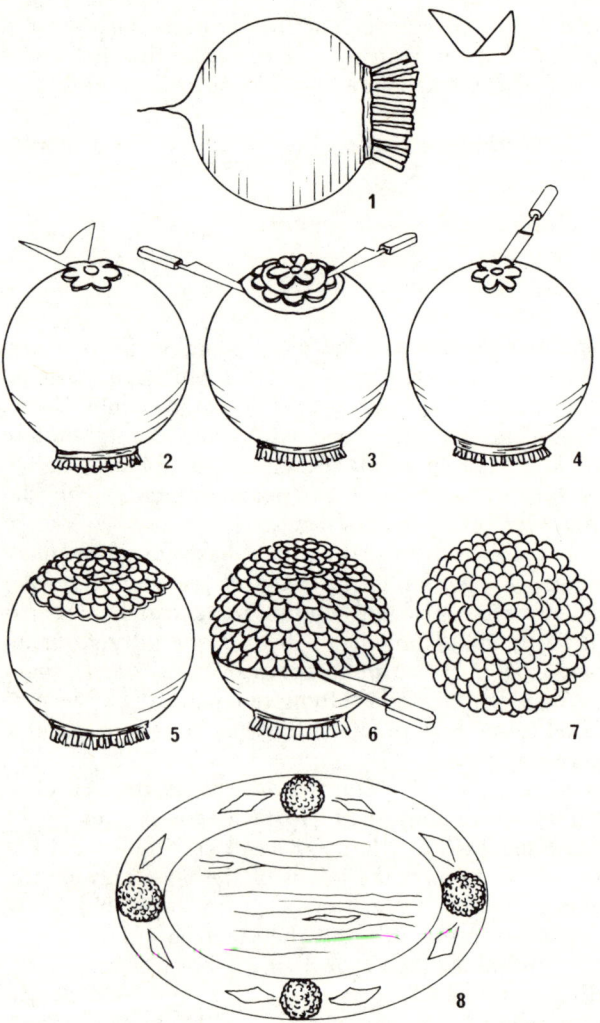

Figure 5.2 A decorative azalea blossom may be carved from a turnip without too much difficulty. A small piece of tin can, bent into a V shape, or a V-shaped wood-

end so that the vegetable will sit straight on the platter. Cut a ¼-inch strip from around the top of the vegetable. Then cut five petals around the outside by cutting down toward the base but not through it. Then remove a very thin section of the vegetable between these petals and the central part. Round off the central part, and remove the trimmings made in rounding it. Cut five more petals between the first petals cut in the central part, making them smaller than the first and not cutting as deeply. Continue this procedure until the center is reached. With the point of a knife, twist the center petals carefully to open the rose.

Beet or turnip azaleas Using a small V-shaped piece of tin can or a V wood-carving chisel, make a tiny cut in the very top of the peeled vegetable, so that a miniscule flap (a petal) is created. Make a lot of these cuts all around the top of the vegetable; the whole series will be the size of a dime. Remove a very thin portion of flesh between the petals and the main part of the vegetable. Make another series, a little larger, staggering the petals under the first series and adding several petals to the row if necessary. Remove another thin slice from under this row. Continue the procedure until half the vegetable has been scalloped. Cut the "flower" away from the base.

---

carving chisel will do the job (see diagrams 1 and 4). Cut a series of tiny flaps, or petals, around the top of the peeled vegetable, making the whole series about the size of a dime (diagrams 2 and 4). With a sharp knife, remove a very thin layer of flesh from beneath the petals (3) and form a second series of petals, slightly larger than the first, staggering the flaps and adding more if necessary. Repeat these processes until half the vegetable has been carved. Then remove flower from base (6). Diagram 7 is an overhead view of the finished blossom and diagram 8 illustrates how it can be used as platter decoration. (Adapted from August Forster, *American Culinary Art*, Ahrens Publishing Company, Inc., New York, 1951, 1958.)

Timbales Aspic molds make attractive feature decorations for platters. They can range from molds suitable for decorating individual plates—that is, 2 to 3 ounces—to pint and quart molds. Numerous decorated shapes are available, but plain forms with fancy contents are much more common.

Even a mold filled merely with brightly colored gelatin and suspended over evenly cut and brightly colored garnish looks attractive. Most professional timbales, however, are more formal. When the gelatin is turned from the mold, there is an elaborate geometric or floral pattern on the bottom and sides made from cutouts (see major pieces above) of vegetables. The process has three steps:

1 The mold is first lined with clear gelatin to hold the cutouts and to protect them when the gelatin is slightly heated to remove it from the mold. Then it is chilled.
2 The very thin cutouts are carefully placed in the mold by dipping them on the end of a toothpick in liquid gelatin. Then the mold is chilled again.
3 The mold is then filled with almost completely gelled gelatin so that it will not wash away the cutouts. Then the mold is chilled once more before all the gelatin is removed.

There are two tricks to the process. The mold must be lined properly with about 3/16 of an inch of gelatin. First the mold is chilled to the rim in a pan of ice and water without allowing the water to wash into the mold. Then the gelatin, at an almost syrupy consistency, is poured into the mold to fill it while it is still in the water. The instant the layer forms, the mold is removed from the water, the still-liquid gelatin is dumped from it, and the mold is twirled so that the gelatin is evenly spread on the walls and bottom. While twirling the mold, it should be held by the rim because finger contact will create a warm spot that will not take as much gelatin.

Getting the gelatin unmolded is the second trick. After it is well chilled, slide a thin sharp knife around the rim to a depth of ¼ inch to break the seal. Then, dip it for 5 seconds in warm water. Tap the bottom while holding it over a plate at a slight angle (not flush with the plate) and it should fall out.

Instead of clear gelatin, the cutout decoration can be made of white or colored chaudfroid. The general practice is to make a geometric design, for example a checkerboard pattern of concentric circles or diamonds in the center, and to repeat the pattern in a band around the sides. As some guest is likely to sample the mold, it should be made edible by using well-flavored gelatin and cooked garnish items. It does not have to be a taste treat, since whoever eats the decorations of a platter does so at his own risk.

Fruit Decorations Decorative items made from small fruits such as oranges, lemons, and even small grapefruit are perfectly suited to garnishing an individual customer's plate. Large fruits, such as pineapples, melons, and coconuts, are better suited to platters.

The potential of large fruits is fairly obvious, because once they have been hollowed out, they can be filled with edible decorative items: fruit balls, berries, pickles, sauces, salads, and so on.

The most common treatment is a basket. Level off the fruit—a melon, for example—by cutting a thin slice from the bottom. Draw an outline of the basket and handle on the top half of the fruit. Cut into the melon with a knife (a small keyhole saw would be needed for a coconut) to remove the extraneous upper sections. Care must be taken not to cut into the section that will form the handle. Remove the fruit beneath the handle—leaving only the husk, or rind, of the fruit to form the handle. Scoop out the meat in the bottom

58 ADDING EYE APPEAL TO FOODS

Figure 5.3 To make a melon basket, suitable for platter decoration, cut a thin slice from the bottom of the fruit to form a flat surface. Outline the handle and the edge of

half of the basket. The handle and the edge of the basket can be cut in a zigzag fashion to create a notched edge, if desired.

The fruit can also be topped so that the top sixth becomes a cover that can be propped at an angle—with toothpicks, perhaps—on the edge of the base. The topping cut can also be serrated.

Arrangement of the Buffet

Choice of Items

The first imperative of buffet planning must be its adequacy as a meal or a significant part of a meal. The guest will not be so overwhelmed by the beauty of the buffet that he will forget that he came to the restaurant to eat.

In other words, a full-meal buffet must offer selections in each course category: appetizers, hot and cold main dishes, salads, breads, desserts, and baked goods. Selection from items of equal taste appeal and cost can then be made on the basis of visual effect.

---

the basket and cut away rind and fruit, using caution to avoid cutting into the handle (diagram 1). Remove fruit from under the handle and from the main body of the melon. Attractive effects are achieved by forming a rounded handle (2); making a series of small holes with cutter (3); scalloping the handle and edge of basket (4); or using a zigzag design to edge two handles and the border (5). A zigzag wedge cut from a melon as in figure 6 results in a crib shape suitable for use at a baby shower. The wheels can be cut from a rutabaga and attached with toothpicks. Diagram 7 shows a honeydew melon with fancy scalloped border and scenery carved in the main body of the fruit. (Adapted from August Forster, *American Culinary Art*, Ahrens Publishing Company, Inc., New York, 1951, 1958.)

Three rules are often pivotal in planning buffets:

1. Make the color of the food items a primary consideration; avoid having too many items of the same color wherever possible.
2. Avoid the repetition of major food items as garnishes or main courses. For example, don't use citrus fruits on more than one platter. Do not have two meatball dishes unless the buffet is huge.
3. Vary the type of preparation so that the form and texture of the food appear different. Avoid too many chopped salads, mixed meat and vegetable combinations, or mounds of food in mayonnaise.

Position of Plates and Platters

If a buffet will be approached from only one side, then that end of the buffet must have plates on it. A double line buffet, for more people, requires plates on both ends. The position of food items on the buffet, unless it represents a single course, follows the order of the meal, even if hot dishes and desserts are on separate islands.

Even though people will be carrying their entire selection back to their tables on a single plate and they can eat it in any order they please, to avoid being visually disruptive, the operator should order the buffet with appetizer items first, main dish items second, and salads last.

Most buffets look best with oval platters positioned in a herringbone pattern, angled so that they point to the center of the buffet, which contains a major piece. Circular platters seem to suit the middle ground of a buffet approached from the front. It is also possible to make them more visually appealing by placing them on plinths or pedestals made from cloth-covered boxes or cake stands.

A double-tier buffet works well if the table is narrow enough so that an item on the upper tier can be reached without leaning into the potato salad on the bottom one. The upper tier on a wide table should be devoted to decorative elements, including an ice carving that will not be eaten.

If servers are positioned behind the buffet, a wide table can be filled with food. Often servers carve hot items like roast beef or cold items like proscuitto ham. Decorated items that the guest is likely to destroy by serving himself may be given to a server for more careful portioning.

A wall or window against which a buffet may be placed should be covered with a material that coordinates well with the food. Thick drapes are a poor choice, but plants several feet behind the buffet and in front of the wall or a mirror are excellent.

Eye Appeal for Salads

There are hors d'oeuvre, main-course, garnish, salad course, and dessert salads. Whatever its role, the salad's appeal depends considerably on its appearance, however excellent the flavor of the ingredients or the dressing. When a salad is an appetizer—mixed vegetables in mayonnaise (*salade à la Russe*), for example—it must first look appetizing to taste appetizing. As a garnish or an accompanying course, a salad's major purpose is to enhance the appearance of either the main dish or the table. Dessert salads that follow the main meal, such as fruit chunks in sauce, must invite the already full diner to eat by their eye appeal.

The cook or the restaurateur instructing him has essentially three opportunities to add visual appeal to salads of any sort:

1. The choice and preparation of main salad elements
2. The choice and preparation of salad garnish elements
3. The preparation of the salad itself in the serving vessel

Main Salad Elements

There are almost 100 fresh fruits and vegetables available from commercial sources in the United States, and any of them can be used in salads. Proper preparation of these elements is vitally important to their appearance. Although some are best as garnishes —limes and lemons for example—most can be attractively processed to become main ingredients in various types of salad:

> Anise Trim and remove leaves from bulb, cut bulb into thin strips or separate into leaves. Store in cold water. Color: pale green.
>
> Apples Wash and peel or leave unpeeled. Cut into wedges, rings, or dice. Color: white without peel, red, yellow, or green and white with peel.
>
> Apricots Blanch to remove skins, separate into halves to remove pits. Color: orange-pink.
>
> Artichokes Whole artichokes may be used raw if they are under 1 inch in size. Otherwise, cook or use canned artichoke bottoms or halves, soaked to remove brine. Color: pale yellow-green.
>
> Asparagus Cook; use neatly trimmed whole spears, tips, or cut sections. Color: bright green.
>
> Avocados Halve to remove pit. Use whole halves or peel and cut wedges, slices, balls with melon scoop, or dice. Store in lemon juice and water to prevent discoloration.
>
> Bananas Peel; cut into slices, strips, wedges, or sections; store in lemon juice and water to prevent discoloration. Color: pale yellow.
>
> Beans Young, tiny snap beans can be used raw; otherwise, trim and cook taking care to preserve bright green color; or, use frozen products. Color: bright green.
>
> Beets Water-cook fresh beets; then peel; or, use canned beets. Cut in slices, use metal cutouts, cut julienne strips, or use small beets whole.
>
> Beet leaves Young small leaves can be washed and used raw as a green, like spinach.

Berries   Raspberries, blueberries, boysenberries, and others should be picked to remove bruised fruit and stems. Color: red, purple, green, blue, or black.

Broccoli   Flowerettes of fresh, young broccoli can be used raw; or, cook, trim, and cut evenly. Or use cooked frozen spears or chopped broccoli. Color: bright green.

Cabbage   Trim, chop, grate, or cut into strips. Color: dark green, light green, or red, depending on type.

Carrots   Peel; use raw or cooked; chopped, sliced, grated, cut in julienne. Color: bright orange.

Cauliflower   Fresh cauliflower flowerettes can be used raw, trimmed from head, or cooked and cut into flowerettes. Or, use cooked frozen vegetables. Color: white.

Celeriac   Trim; peel; cut into thin slices, julienne, or decorative shapes.

Celery   Trim; remove strings; cut into slices, strips, or special shapes. Use raw, cooked, or partially cooked. Color: pale green.

Cherries   Stone (there are special tools and small machines available). Use whole or halved without stem. Color: deep red.

Chinese cabbage   Trim; cut into slices, strips, squares, etc. Color: pale yellow-green.

Coconuts   Grate fresh meat. Store in cold water. Color: white.

Sweet corn   Kernels of fresh corn may be used raw or water cooked. Use stripped kernels or sections cut through cob. Color: bright yellow or pale yellow.

Cranberries   Wash, pick for bad berries. Use raw or cooked. Color: bright red.

Cucumbers Trim; use peeled, unpeeled, or partially peeled to make decoration. Cut into slices, or seed and cut into dice, wedges, slices, or balls (with melon baller). Color: light green or dark green and light green.

Eggplant Very young, tender, small eggplants can be used raw (in moderation); or, bake or steam. Use peeled or unpeeled in wedges, slices, sticks, or dice. Color: light green, purple, or white (from white eggplant) and light green.

Endive Belgian endive. Cut into strips, rounds, or separate leaves. Store in lemon juice and water to prevent discoloration.

Escarole Trim, wash, and cut into bite-sized pieces.

Figs Halve or quarter. Color: green or deep purple.

Grapefruit Section or cut "supremes". Color: bright yellow or pale pink.

Grapes Separate into clusters or single berries. Use half or whole, peeled or unpeeled. Color: green, red, or purple, depending on type.

Greens Mustard, turnip, or collard greens. Wash, trim carefully. Color: dark green.

Leeks Wash and trim. May be used raw or water cooked. Cut white part and tender leaf area into slices, strips, or dice. Color: bright green and white.

Lettuce The visual appeal of the various types of lettuce is in the shape of the leaves.

> Bibb Small, fragile, yellow-green, soft leaves.
>
> Boston Like Bibb, but with larger leaves.
>
> Bronze Long, soft leaves with crumpled edges fringed with reddish bronze.

Chicory (curly endive) Feathery leaves, green and white-yellow.

Field lettuce Small spears on tiny stems.

Iceberg Large, light white leaves.

Leaf lettuce Long, soft leaves with crumpled edges.

Oak leaf Soft, fuzzy, pale green leaves, shaped like oak leaves.

Romaine Long, oval, dark green leaves.

Mangoes Peel; remove pit by halving. Cut fresh into wedges or sticks. Color: pale yellow to bright orange.

Melons Use wedges with skins, or peel and cut into strips, dice, or slices. Or, use melon scoop to make balls. Color: pink, yellow, green, or red, depending on type.

Mushrooms Mushrooms may be used raw. Use tiny caps, tiny whole mushrooms, julienne or large mushrooms, slices, quarters, and so on. Keep in lemon juice and water to prevent discoloration. Color: white-brown.

Nectarines Peel by blanching, or use unpeeled. Remove pit by halving; use whole halves, or cut into slices or wedges. Color: yellow or blush-red and yellow.

Okra Small okra may be used raw, or water cooked until just tender. Use whole. Color: pale green.

Onions Peel; cut into rings, slices, dice, strips, and so on. Color: white or red.

Green onions Trim. Cut into slices. Color: bright green and white.

Oranges Peel. Cut into segments or slices. Color: orange.

Papaya   Cut in half. Remove seeds; cut balls with melon scoop, or peel and cut in slices or wedges. Color: pale yellow to orange.

Parsley   Use flowers only. Color: bright green.

Parsnips   Water cook and peel. Cut into slices, dice, decorative shapes, and so on. Color: pale yellow-orange.

Peaches   Peel by blanching, or use unpeeled. Remove pit by halving; use whole halves, or cut into slices or wedges. Color: yellow or blush-red and yellow.

Pears   Peel with potato peeler, or use unpeeled. Cut in half to remove core, or use apple corer. Cut in wedges, halves, slices, dice, strips, sticks, and so on. Or, use canned pears. Color: pale yellow, green, or red, depending on type.

Peas   Remove from pod. Use whole or in halves. Color: pale green or yellow.

Snow peas   Remove leaf and string (like string beans); use small whole pods raw, or cook. Color: bright green.

Peppers   Trim off stem end. Cut in half to remove seeds. Cut in strips, dice, decorative shapes, rings (without halving), and so on. Color: bright green or bright red.

Persimmons   Peel carefully by hand. Cut carefully into slices or wedges. Color: bright orange-red.

Pineapples   Trim leaves and outer skin. Remove inner light core. Cut meat into wedges, sections, chunks, strips, or sticks. Keep in lemon juice and water to prevent discoloration. Or, use canned chunks, rings, sections, spears, or crushed. Color: bright yellow or pale yellow.

Pomegranates Cut fruit in half. Carefully remove seeds (the desired part) from surrounding pulp. Color: bright purple-red.

Plums Peel by blanching, or use unpeeled. Halve to remove pits. Use whole halves, or quarter. Color: green, red, purple, or yellow, depending on type.

Potatoes Peel, cook, and cut into rounds, slices, balls, wedges, strips, dice, and so on. Or, peel, cut, and then cook. Color: white.

Radishes Trim off stem and root ends. Cut into rounds, slices, balls (with melon scoop); or, use whole halves or quarters. Color: red and white.

Rhubarb String like celery. Trim. Cut into slices or dice and water cook until just tender. Color: bright pink-red.

Spinach Fresh, young spinach may be used as a salad green. Wash, trim, and cut away from stems. Color: dark green.

Squash Trim, slice, water cook until just tender. Color: green or yellow, depending on type.

Strawberries Hull; use whole, in halves, in quarters, or in slices. Color: bright red.

Sweet potatoes Water cook or bake. Remove peel; cut into dice, slices, wedges, or decorative shapes. Color: bright orange.

Tangerines Peel; separate into segments. Color: bright orange.

Tomatoes Peel by blanching, or use unpeeled. Trim stem end. Cut into wedges, slices, dice, or chunks. Color: bright red or yellow.

Cherry tomatoes Remove stems; use whole or in halves. Color: bright red.

Watercress Trim stems short. Color: dark green.

Garnish Elements

Garnish elements for salads add visual appeal by increasing the color and texture values of the salad; they improve the taste; and they add food value—the addition of meat and cheese, for example, makes a salad a main course.

Just as almost anything can be a salad, almost anything—from cold, cooked vegetables to edible flowers—can be a salad garnish. Some garnishes are especially popular because of their appearance, their texture, and, frequently, their flavor:

> Aspic cubes Colored cubes of gelatin with fruit, meat, or wine flavors.
>
> Bacon Crumbled, crisp, fried bacon.
>
> Bread Fried croutons in squares, cubes, or cutout decorative shapes.
>
> Caviar Red or black caviar as a final topping.
>
> Capers Small (nonpareil) whole capers, or larger chopped capers.
>
> Cheese Any kind of cheese: cubed; cutouts; crumbled; grated; sliced; or julienne.
>
> Cutouts Pieces of vegetables and meats cut out with a truffle or aspic cutter, both of which resemble small cookie cutters.
>
> Dressings A dressing can contain a finely chopped attractive garnish, such as green and red pepper, or be colorful itself: thousand island, green goddess, blue cheese, and others.
>
> Dried fruit Raisins, currants, sultanas, chopped apricots, figs, or prunes can be used in salads as they come from the package, chopped as necessary, or rehydrated with warm water.
>
> Eggs Hard-cooked eggs can be used in many attractive ways: sieved, diced, or chopped, both whites and yolks; in slices, wedges, halves,

quarters, or sixths, and so on. Scrambled eggs may be cut in julienne; poached eggs can be the central feature of a salad.

Fish Any cooked fish can be cut into chunks or flakes. Preserved fish can supply color interest. Try, for example, anchovies, smoked salmon, or herring pieces. Cooked shellfish, such as lobster, shrimp, or crab meat, are all attractive in flakes, slices, whole pieces, or chunks. The restaurateur with an adventurous clientele might try raw fish. Raw tuna, for example, is a beautiful marbleized pink.

Frozen and canned vegetables Instead of using only fresh ones, try frozen or canned vegetables as attractive salad elements. Many vegetables that cannot be used raw are available in cans: kidney beans, chick peas, and artichoke bottoms are just a few.

Herbs Although chopped herbs of any sort make a salad attractive, whole sprigs of mint, dill, parsley, or sweet basil add flavor as well as interest.

Meats Lean, thin-sliced meats of all types have a definite place in salads, especially when cut attractively in lozenges, julienne strips, dice, small squares, and parallelograms. Consider using white- and dark-meat chicken or turkey; pink pickled tongue, ham, and corned beef, or light veal.

Nuts Nuts generally add texture and flavor: try slivered, sliced, or chopped almonds; hazelnuts, walnuts, peanuts, pecans, and others. Pistachios add color (green) as well.

Olives Black, green, and green stuffed olives—either pitted and whole or sliced, diced, or chopped—are cliché and no longer add much salad interest, but they are still useful in moderate quantities.

Pickles   Pickles of all types offer added color and texture: julienne, chopped, or sliced gherkins; pickle chips; pickle relish; pickled cauliflower, carrots, onions, watermelon, or peppers, and so on.

Popcorn   Can be used in place of croutons.

Truffles   Even though sliced, ripe, black olives give the same visual appeal, truffles are required in some classical salads.

Assembling Salads

Visual Elements of a Salad

A salad is made up of four visual elements:

1. The accessorization: the dish, bowl, or plate to be used
2. The liner on the dish or bowl
3. The main elements of the salad itself
4. The topping or garnish

Items carefully chosen for each of these elements—on the basis of their color, texture, form, and size—give definite eye appeal to salads. Obviously, taste suitability is a consideration, but it is less of a factor than might be thought, as the restaurateur is never in a situation where he must combine such incompatible ingredients as smoked mussels and pineapple, or rhubarb and parsnips. He is developing an attractive and tasteful salad at the same time, or he is garnishing a tasteful salad, and among all the alternatives of main elements and garnishes, good sense should lead him away from such obvious mismatches.

Accessorization As salads themselves are colorful and interestingly textured, accessorization can be simple: Use salad plates or wooden or glass bowls.

Liners Most composed salads look most attractive when the main elements are not placed directly on the plate. Most of the time a lettuce leaf of some sort suffices as a liner. It is also possible to build a salad on top of a piece of sliced pineapple; within a fringe or curly endive, on top of sliced cucumbers, sliced tomatoes, or chopped vegetables; or even on a plate well filled with colored aspic. The most obvious exception is the salad of chopped greens that, in effect, is its own liner for the topping, garnish, or dressing used.

Main elements of the salad The possible number of combinations of salad elements and garnishes is truly astronomical, even if the restaurateur were restricted to the items identified above. They can be used 3, 4, or even 30 at a time.

Color, form, and texture are the main considerations. The most attractive classical salads offer these in variety. Here are three examples: Salade à la Russe is composed of diced pink ham, julienne-cut red tongue, rounds of red and white sausage, slivered green pickles, wedges of green and white cucumber, cut green beans, green peas, strips of brown anchovies, diced red and green peppers, round green capers in vinegar and oil, with a spot of black caviar on top. Salade Suédoise, is made of lozenges of brown, thin-sliced cooked beef, diced white potatoes, julienne of red beets, diced red and white apples, garnished with raw grey oysters, and hard-cooked yellow and white egg. Salade Nicoise is a mixture of pink tuna fish chunks, red tomatoes and pimiento, black olives, red peppers, green peppers, chopped onions, green capers, pickles, anchovies, chopped herbs, and egg slices.

If every restaurateur would consider the more common chef's salad or antipasto as a model, selecting salad ingredients for their visual appeal would pose no problems.

Topping and garnishes Salads can have the equivalent of the cherry on top of the ice cream sundae, a little touch that really adds nothing to the item, but seems to bring it all together; a focus for the eye. Often this can simply be a garnish element that gives the salad a feeling of composition by being in the center or on top. For example, a salad can seem to be assembled around or under a slice of hard-cooked egg. Almost anything in the middle of a mound improves its appearance, like the spot of caviar in the salade à la Russe, or even a star cut from a black olive in the middle of a mound of potato salad.

Rules for Building a Salad

1. Choose items on the basis of color, texture, form, and size.
2. Make sure that each item is in perfect condition, that greens have been washed and crisped in ice water and then dried, that moist foods have been drained, and so on.
3. Cut each food as evenly as possible into dice, julienne strips (the size of a double matchstick), balls, slices, lozenges, or whatever shape you need. Irregularity disrupts the visual impression.
4. Keep items separated until just before the salad must be assembled for the customer, so that flavors do not become mixed and the elements do not mush together. Always reserve toppings until the last moment so that they give the salad a very fresh appearance.
5. Use chilled plates so that greens do not wilt.
6. When building the salad in a plate or bowl, allow the margin of the vessel to show to frame the

salad. Trim or cut the liner as necessary to look neat.

7. Build the salad with a definite back and front (which will face the customer).
8. Aim to make a mounded, rather than a flat, plate.
9. In making a composed salad (one that is not mixed), use odd numbers of elements (three, five, or seven, rather than two, four, or six), and balance the plate with articles of the same size on opposite sides or a symmetry of forms or in another decorative arrangement.
10. Even when using many ingredients, do not crowd the plate. Keep it simple and natural looking, casual but not studied, even though it has been carefully designed.

Eye Appeal for Cold Plates

Cold meat platters, diet plates, cold seafood plates, and sandwich platters are part of many restaurant menus. Visual appeal is extremely important in making the food appetizing, as there are no fragrant aromas wafting up to the customer from a cold plate. Cold plate main items also often look less inviting when the customer mentally compares them with the same items as hot entrées. Sliced leg of lamb is a good example, or a cold platter of fried chicken.

The visual appeal of cold platters is a combination of attractive garnishing and decoration and plate composition, including the preparation of the main items.

Garnishes and Decoration

The restaurateur has an abundant variety of inexpensive, easy-to-use garnishes in preparing cold platters. And they can be very appealing; no one is obliged to use a pickle wedge and potato chips or a paper soufflé cup of day-old coleslaw. Garnishes and decorations may be considered in categories:

1. Vegetable and fruit vessels
2. Decorations from the pastry bag
3. Preserved fruits
4. Pickles
5. Snack products
6. Vegetable and fruit decorations

Vegetable and Fruit Vessels

Apples, oranges, lemons, cucumbers, and tomatoes make excellent decorative holders for relishes, cold sauces, vegetable salads, and chopped or shredded main cold plate items. Some good examples are: a tomato stuffed with crab salad, an orange basket filled with pickle relish, a cucumber boat filled with dilled shrimp, or a lemon basket filled with cranberry sauce.

Hollowed vegetables and fruits The most basic design for a vegetable or fruit vessel is simply the hollowed out fruit or vegetable. The top is removed carefully about 1/6 of the way down with a sharp paring knife, and then the fruit is emptied with a teaspoon or melon scoop.

Cutting the top off by making a zigzag cut considerably improves the appearance of an orange, apple, lemon, or tomato. Using a sharp paring knife with the blade held at a 45-degree angle, make a ¼-inch cut to the center of the fruit. Then turn the knife so that the second cut makes a V with the first. Make another V with the third cut on the same line, and continue around the fruit, cutting to the center each time. Separate the top from the bottom, and hollow out the fruit or vegetable. If the cuts are made in the exact center instead of over the top, the two halves, with notched edges, can become attractive decorations themselves without being hollowed out. Top them with a colorful bit of fruit or vegetable, such as a maraschino cherry.

Fruit baskets Fruit baskets can be made from grapefruit, lemons, or oranges. They are often filled with fruit or colorful relishes. Make a flat end to the fruit by cutting a thin slice from the blossom end so that it will stand straight on the platter. Draw an outline of the basket and the handle on the top half of the fruit. Cut into the fruit with a sharp paring knife to remove the extraneous upper sections. Care must be taken not to cut into the section that will form the handle. Remove the fruit beneath the handle, leaving only the rind of the fruit to form the handle. Scoop out the meat in the bottom half of the basket. A more visually interesting handle will result if zigzag cuts—rather than straight lines—are used on both sides of the handle and on the top edge of the basket.

Fruit crown A fruit crown, which resembles a small vase with a zigzag top, is easily made from an orange, lemon, or grapefruit. Soak the fruit in warm water until the skin softens. Then make a knife cut through the skin (only the skin) midway between the stem and blossom ends. Or, peel a strip from this area with a channel cutter. Carefully roll the skin inside out, away from the cuts. You may insert a teaspoon under the skin, but be careful not to damage the fruit, which is the center of the vase. Make zigzag cuts on the top of the upper half of the skin to form the "crown."

Cucumber basket Cut a thin strip from the bottom of a firm, medium-sized cucumber using a sharp knife or a vegetable peeler. With the paring knife, either make zigzag cuts or, more easily, simply cut off the top third of the cucumber and notch or scallop the cut surfaces. Hollow out the cucumber with a melon scoop or sharp teaspoon so that a basket is formed.

Decorations from the Pastry Bag

A cold platter can be decorated with a pastry bag and tube filled with some tasty semisolid, such as mayonnaise with a little gelatin, a dip, a spread, or flavored butter that can be piped onto the food items themselves or onto the plate. A cold plate of smoked salmon, for example, could benefit handsomely from a rosette of cream cheese or butter made with a pastry bag and a star tube. Or, a ripple of dilled mayonnaise could zigzag across smoked trout.

In addition, hollowed out cherry tomatoes, cucumber barrels, or mushroom caps could be filled with cheddar cheese spread from a pastry bag. Rolled ham slices could be finished with spicy bean puree in the hollow ends.

Preserved Fruits

Most canned fruits and a few dried ones make attractive additions to cold plates. Two fruits can be used together—a crab apple in a pineapple ring, for example—or the fruit can be combined with another food—a large, dried prune might be filled with cheese or relish.

Unlike other garnishes for cold plates, which require some labor involvement, most canned fruits are "dump out" items: They can be placed on plates exactly as they come from the cans. The restaurateur who wants to distinguish his operation from an institutional one using fruit directly from the can might consider using some unusual secondary garnishes. A canned pear half is not particularly noteworthy, but a canned pear half filled with pink, shredded ginger is. Here are some more examples.

1. Spiced apple rings sandwiched between yellow and green pineapple rings
2. Apricot halves filled with red pepper relish
3. Pitted cherries in a sweet-and-sour pickle sauce in half a green pickled tomato
4. Figs marinated in a spicy pickle
5. Grapes mixed with maraschino cherry halves
6. Peaches filled with chutney
7. Pears with julienne of prosciutto ham

8   Pineapple chunks and watermelon pickles
9   Purple plum halves filled with chowchow
10 Stewed prunes with bacon bean paste

Pickles and Preserved Vegetables

Pickles and olives are standard cold plate garnishes; without doubt, they add eye appeal. Unfortunately, many restaurateurs fail to create unique as well as attractive plates because they use only the "usual" pickles.

In addition to pickle chips; dill cuts; sweet mixed pickles; gherkins; midget pickles; and black, green, and pimiento-stuffed green olives, which are aggressively promoted by major companies and marketing boards, there are hundreds of attractive pickled and preserved vegetables that are available and *different.* Consider these: baby eggplant stuffed with pimiento; tiny pickled pears; peppers stuffed with sauerkraut; Italian peppers with bread stuffing; banana peppers; Tuscan peppers; Jalapeno peppers; pickled watermelon rind; jardinière salad; almond-stuffed olives; anchovy-stuffed olives; and pickled walnuts.

Not only are these items decorative, they are tasty and fairly unusual, although they are readily available from commercial institutional suppliers. If your present distributors do not carry them, distributors catering to ethnic restaurants—Greek, Italian, or Hungarian—will.

In addition, several lines of pickle products are distributed throughout the United States; these products feature a number of pickled "salads" such as three-bean salad and corn relish, varieties of mixed vegetables, and individual pickled items such as dilled Brussels sprouts, onion rings, cauliflower, and the like. These, like preserved vegetables, are "dump out" items that require no extra labor whatsoever to supply visual interest.

Snack Products

The only good thing about potato chips as a plate garnish is that they cover a great deal of the plate for a fairly small cost. They are not particularly attractive, however, especially when they have been broken in handling.

When plate coverage is not a problem, these other snack products offer better flavor, increased eye appeal, and variety: any of the extruded brand-name chips, twists, circles, cartwheels, or bowties; pretzels in about 30 varieties; unsweetened dried breakfast cereals, seasoned and toasted in the oven; or nuts of any type.

Candy can also decorate a cold plate. Although it may seem odd at first to garnish a cold meat platter with striped peppermints, customer reaction is excellent, and the flavor of the mints is no less compatible with the meat than mint jelly is with lamb. Of course, the customer may simply eat them later.

Vegetable Decorations

Vegetable decorations involve some labor. Fortunately though, no great skill is required to make a tomato rose or to hollow out an inch-thick peeled slice of cucumber and fill it with shredded carrots. Most decorations of this sort keep several days if held in ice water in the refrigerator. Kitchen personnel can make them during idle moments and use them as necessary during rush periods. Problems occur only when the kitchen has not completely prepared itself for service and someone must start making pickle fans while turning out a sandwich every 30 seconds.

Radish flowers and figures The "mock" rose, made from a radish, has itself become stylized by sloppy workmen. For a *rose*, five definite petals are cut; then a thin slice must be cut between the petals and the round center of the radish if it is to look at all like a flower. Other flowers can be cut from radishes: *Radish tulip:* Cut a thin slice from each end of the radish. Cut four petals around the outside, but do not cut through the base. (Note that the rose has five petals, the tulip has four.) Remove a thin slice between each petal and the inner section. Cut an X in the top of the center. (The X will open up when the radish is held in ice water.) *Wild rose:* Follow the procedure above, but instead of an X, carve out three very small V-shaped notches across the center of the top; then carve three more notches perpendicular to the first notches, creating a grid-like effect. *Rosebud:* Leave a small piece of stem and root on the radish. Cut four petals from the root end to the stem end but do not cut through the base. Peel the skin from the center section only, leaving a small bit at the base. *Radish cups:* Cut a thin slice from the root end, and leave a small piece of stem on the radish. Make five zigzag cuts (a total of 10 cuts) all the way around the middle of the radish. Separate the halves. *Radish fan:* Cut the radish in half lengthwise from the root end to the stem end. Cut off the stem; leave a very small portion of the root. Cut very thin slices in the radish half from stem to root end, but do not cut through the root end.

Cucumber Decorations *Scored slices:* Using either a fork or a channel cutter, strip pieces of cucumber peel in parallel rows from a whole cucumber; then cut into slices. *Notched wheels:* Cut five ¼-inch deep, V-shaped notches down the whole length of the cucumber and remove the cut pieces; then cut the cucumber into slices. *Twists:* cut a small slit halfway through a decorated or undecorated slice; hold each end and twist into an S-shape. *Barelles:* Cut inch-thick slices of scored or peeled cucumber. Shape the top and bottom slightly by removing enough vegetable to bevel them slightly. Seed the cucumber, and fill the center with shredded carrots, thin radishes, or pickle relish. *Rings:* Hollow out a peeled or scored cucumber with a sharp knife, and cut it into rings. Use it as is, or link the rings by making a small cut in each and joining one to the other.

Lemon Decorations *Scored slices:* With a channel cutter, strip pieces of the lemon peel in parallel rows the length of a whole lemon; then cut into slices. *Twists:* Cut a small slit halfway through a scored or unscored slice; hold each end and twist into an S shape. *Peeled slices:* Soak a lemon in hot water to loosen the skin. Make a knife cut through the skin (but not the meat) midway between stem and blossom ends, or remove a strip of peel around the center with a channel cutter. With a spoon inserted underneath it, remove the skin. Cut the lemon into thin slices. Dip one half of each slice into paprika or parsley, or, holding the slice between thumb and forefinger, belly out a portion and dip it so that a strip of paprika or parsley is made down the middle.

Carrot decorations *Wheels:* With channel cutter or a sharp knife, make five deep parallel grooves the length

Figure 7.1. Carrot flowers make colorful accents for a buffet platter or as part of a floral centerpiece.

Peel a large carrot and cut it lengthwise into thin, wide rectangles from 3 to 5 inches long.

Make five equidistant slits in the rectangle, running lengthwise, and starting about half an inch from each end (1).

Cut each outside section of the rectangle exactly in half, leaving "petal" free to curl.

Fold carrot slice and fasten with toothpick (2).

Slit and fold five slices of carrot for each flower and thread onto toothpick, one on top of the other, topping the whole with a round slice to form flower center (4). Soak in ice water to curl the petals.

EYE APPEAL FOR COLD PLATES

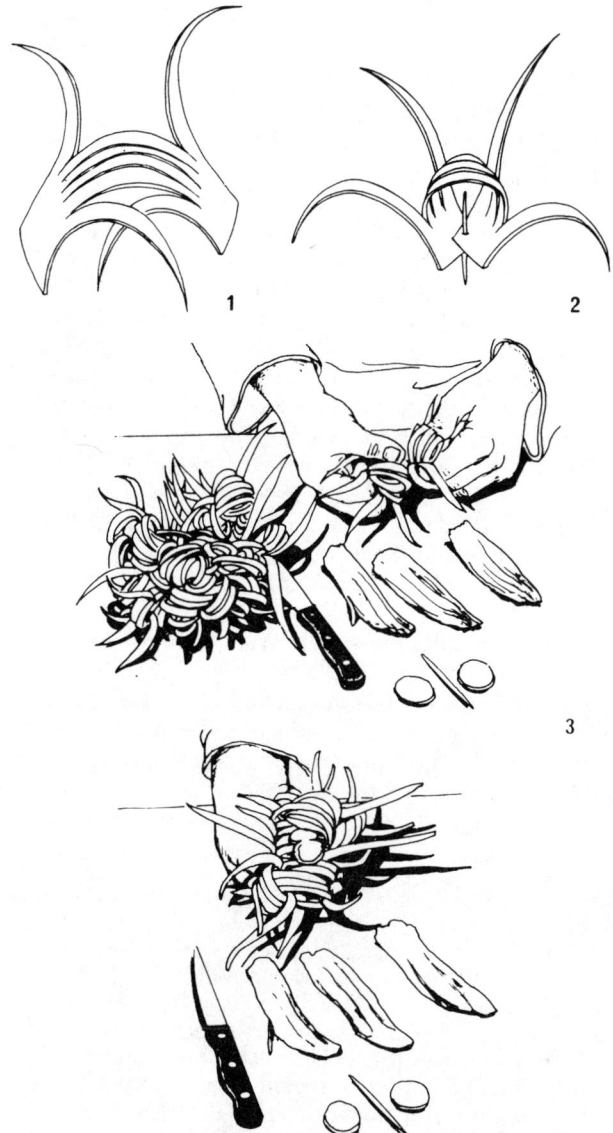

of the carrot. Then slice thinly. *Flowers:* Peel a large carrot, and cut it lengthwise into thin, wide pieces. Trim the slices into rectangles that are approximately 4 inches long and as wide as the size of the carrot allows. Make five equidistant slits in the rectangle, running lengthwise. These slits start and end about ½ inch from either end of the slice. Cut each outer band exactly in half. Bend the carrot rectangle (with two bands cut and four intact) so that the ends meet, and secure the ends with a toothpick. It takes five rectangles to make one flower; each is threaded onto the toothpick, one on top of another. Finally, push a round of carrot onto the toothpick to make the flower's center, and soak the flower in ice water so that the cut ends blossom. *Curls:* Peel a carrot and trim it so that it is approximately the same diameter along its entire length. Place a vegetable peeler at an angle against the flattened root end of the carrot, and turn it so that a spiral cut is made. Soak the curls in ice water and then arrange them on a plate attractively.

Green onion (scallion) flowers Trim a piece of the solid white part of a scallion into a 2- to 3-inch length. Cut parallel ⅛-inch wide strips from either end to the middle, leaving the middle section of the scallion uncut. Press each end (the two cut sections) lightly against the surface of the working area so that the strips spread out to create the flower. Hold the scal-

Figure 7.2. A green onion (scallion) flower is made from a 2- to 3-inch length of the solid white section of the vegetable. Cut away parallel ⅛-inch-wide strips from each end of scallion section, leaving middle part of the length uncut. Press each end lightly against surface of the working area, spreading out the strips to form the flower. Soak in ice water to set. Vary the treatment by first threading the scallion through a large, pitted black olive or through carrot rings.

EYE APPEAL FOR COLD PLATES 85

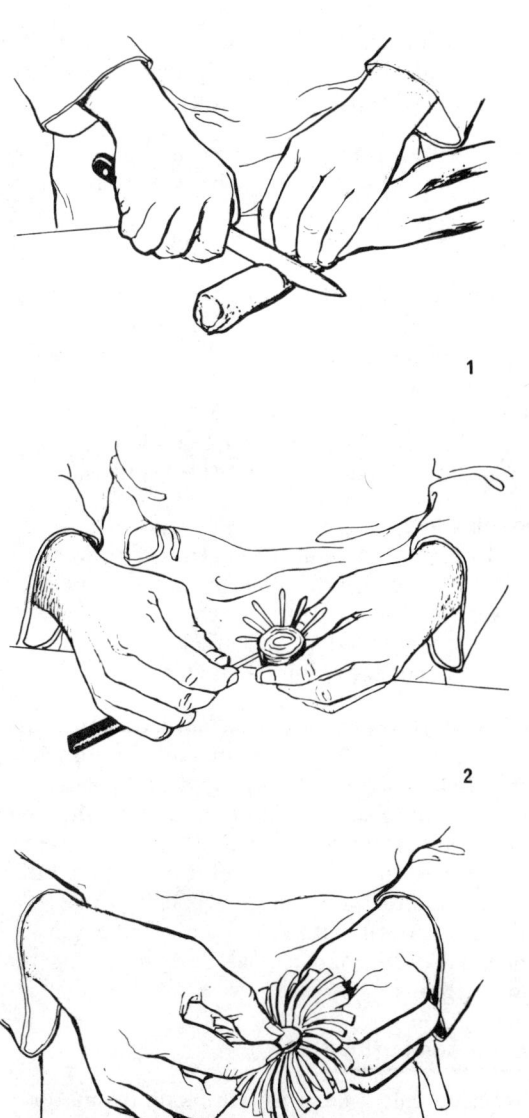

lion in ice water to set the blossom. Vary the treatment by first threading the scallion through a large, pitted black olive or through carrot rings.

Tomato rosette Remove the entire skin of a tomato in a thin, continuous ¾-inch strip as though peeling an apple. Starting with the end removed last, recurl the strip around your finger to make a rose.

Pickle fan Cut a pickle in half lengthwise (use any size from gherkin to kosher dill). In each half, make even parallel slits, not cutting the pickle completely through. The slits may be vertical, with the slices held together by the uncut portion at the top, or horizontal for a featherlike effect. Spread the slices by pressing down on the pickle half to fan them evenly.

Celery pinwheels Trim the leaves from a bunch of celery. Separate the stalks and trim and wash them. Fill each with a colorful cheese spread, and then reconstruct the bunch, starting with the small stalks. Press the stalks together, tie, and chill overnight. Before serving, cut them into thin slices.

Gelatin orange segments Soak an attractive orange in warm water to soften the skin. Cut through the skin midway between the blossom and stem ends with a sharp knife or channel cutter, and carefully remove the skin halves without breaking them, inserting a spoon between the skin and fruit if necessary. Fill each half with gelatin. More than two halves can be prepared with several different colors. When the gelatin has become quite solid, cut as though cutting orange sixths or eighths.

Plate Composition

Attractive cold plates usually contain one or more main elements, one or two vegetable items, and one or more garnishes. As two examples: (1) ham and cheese, coleslaw (with red cabbage) and potato salad (with yellow mayonnaise, red and green peppers), pickle fans, and pickled pears on a lettuce leaf; (2) a split lobster half filled with capers, garnished with a stuffed egg, decorated with mayonnaise piped from a pastry bag, and carrot and leek flowers.

Color, texture, and form in the choice of items are, of course, of paramount importance.

As cold plates are seldom juicy, accessorization can include bread boards, flat basket mats, and even slices of large, round bread (12 inches in diameter).

The major concern in plate composition, other than a balanced arrangement of these items on the plate or serving vessel, is the appearance of the main item itself. Foods such as chicken, lobster, or fish steaks (cold poached salmon, for example) do not present a problem because they are high and therefore look interesting automatically. Sliced meats and cheese, on the other hand, can lose a great deal of their interest because of their flatness.

Most platters are improved if the slices are alternated when two items are used (ham and turkey, for example). Single meats can at least be shingled over each other so that they gain some height. Rolls of meat, even if they must be secured by a frilled tooth-pick, lend the most appeal to a cold platter because they give it some height. Or, the slices of meat may be partially rolled and then shingled by turning a third of the slice under.

Try to look at the platter from the customer's point of view; if it looks interesting and appetizing to you, it will look good to him.

Eye Appeal for Sandwiches

Sandwiches are the mainstays of American restaurants. With the exception of a few dinner restaurants, most operations have some sort of sandwich on their lunch, dinner, supper, and even breakfast menus because customers want them. The operator of a high-check-average restaurant has a problem: How can he make his chicken salad sandwich justify the menu price he needs, when the lunch counter down the street can put as much chicken salad on the bread for a great deal less?

Eye appeal is the answer. A sandwich that looks like it's worth $2.50 *is* worth $2.50, even if the main ingredients cost 45¢ and the lunch counter can afford to sell them at 95¢.

Although the high-check-average restaurant *must* produce eye-appealing sandwiches because of its overhead, other menu items, and reputation, any operation can profit by the same approach. An eye-appealing sandwich is worth more to the drive-in customer, the coffee shop customer, and the lunch-counter customer as well.

In addition to making the sandwich look more appetizing, garnishing and decorative techniques give ordinary sandwiches an excitement that pleases—for example, the customer who likes ham and cheese for lunch but is tired of the ordinary, uninspired ham and cheese sandwich. Make the combination a little more interesting than the kind his mother packed in a brown bag, and he'll be doubly pleased.

Types of Sandwiches

Five types of sandwiches pose individual garnishing and decorating challenges:

1. Closed two-slice sandwiches
2. Triple-deck sandwiches
3. Open-faced sandwiches
4. Sandwiches on exotic breads
5. Fancy sandwiches and canapés

Closed Two-Slice Sandwiches

The primary element in the ordinary closed sandwich's visual appeal is the appearance of quality and value. The bread must be fresh, with a close, smooth texture; the filling should be delicately textured and easy to eat. When the filling contains chopped food, such as tuna fish or hard-cooked egg, the pieces should be large enough to be seen; pasty-looking filling is definitely unattractive. On sandwiches with soft fillings, some crisp vegetable, such as tomato, lettuce, or cucumber, peeking out of the bread, is needed first for visual appeal and height and second for moistness and texture contrast when the sandwich is eaten. When butter is spread on a sandwich, it should be semisoft so that the bread is not torn. Delicatessen sandwiches should be neat and sliced evenly with all the tough and fatty parts of meat trimmed.

Although portion control depends on the operation's costing, a good sandwich is approximately 50 percent bread and 50 percent filling.

Once the operation has a quality sandwich that *looks* like a quality sandwich, the restaurateur can work on further enhancing its appearance.

Figure 8.1. There are several major methods of cutting sandwiches and various ways in which to arrange them on a plate.

EYE APPEAL FOR SANDWICHES 91

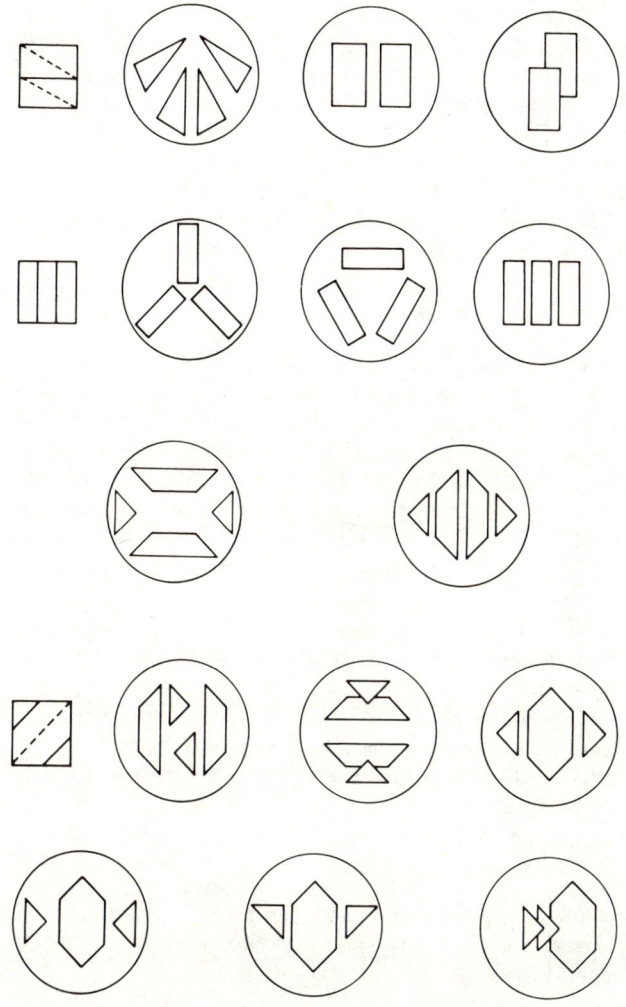

Figure 8.1. (cont'd.) The illustration shows a number of shapes and arrangements frequently used.

Attention should be given to the cutting of the sandwich and its arrangement on the plate. Even with decoration the customer is first struck by the look of the sandwich itself.

As illustrated in Figure 8.1, there are some eight major ways of cutting sandwiches with a number of alternative methods of placing them on plates. Whether crusts are trimmed or left on any sandwich depends primarily on the market's taste.

Triple-Deck Sandwiches

Any sandwich made into a triple-decker immediately becomes more eye appealing, even if the upper deck contains nothing more than lettuce, tomato, and mayonnaise. Any combination sandwich lends itself easily to becoming a triple-deck sandwich: ham and cheese, turkey and salami, or pastrami and corned beef, as well as the familiar club triple-deck sandwich of chicken, bacon, lettuce, tomato, and mayonnaise.

Although triple-deck sandwiches are often cut diagonally in half after being speared with frilled or decorated toothpicks, they are also attractively presented if cut diagonally in quarters and speared by four picks instead of two. The quarters rest on the crust, with points in the air, opening the center of the plate for garnishes.

Open-Faced Sandwiches

There are two types of open-faced sandwiches: the closed sandwich left open and the genuine single-slice open-faced one.

Closed sandwiches left open Rather than close the bread on the most attractive part—the filling—the operator leaves the sandwich open. A good-looking juicy hamburger on a toasted bun criss-crossed by grill marks, with lettuce, tomato, and a slice of onion on the other half of the bun, has more eye appeal than just the top of a bun. Besides, the more plate that is covered, the more substantial the sandwich seems to be.

This approach is, of course, limited to fillings that themselves look attractive, unless they are to be garnished like a genuine single-slice open-faced sandwich or two open-faced sandwiches that are to be slapped together by the customer.

Instead of leaving the whole sandwich open, which almost necessitates leaving the bread whole, half a sandwich might be opened by first cutting it diagonally, arranging it, and then tucking one top quarter under a bottom quarter. A shrimp salad sandwich made this way, for example, would have a quarter exposed that could be decorated with some piped mayonnaise or a single butterfly shrimp.

Single-slice open sandwiches The single-slice open sandwich is a miniature cold plate on a piece of bread that can be so elaborate and generous that the customer may eat the main elements with a fork and ignore the bread.

An open-faced sandwich consists of the bread, which is not cut; usually either butter or mayonnaise to protect it from fillings that are moist; and then the main element, a garnish element, and some attractive topping. The sandwich is built like a banana split. For example, a roast beef sandwich could be composed of a slice of white bread slightly covered with butter and then three thin slices of roast beef, shingled with their ends tucked under to give the sandwich height. A piece of Bibb lettuce might be under the ends of the meat at diagonal corners and a row of thin overlapping tomato slices across the top of the meat from the opposite diagonal corners. Finally, a pickle fan or a little shredded fresh horseradish could top the sandwich.

Since almost any elements may be used, the possibilities for eye appeal are limitless. In addition to the natural attractiveness of the main elements, any minor vegetable decoration, such as radish roses, cucumber or lemon twists, pickles of any type, bits of preserved fruit, or cutouts, can be appropriate on the open-faced sandwich. Simple effects with brilliantly colorful food in the tradition of the Scandinavian originators of the open-faced sandwich are preferred, but there is no reason why a dull item such as meatloaf cannot be more heavily garnished than attractive and expensive shrimp.

Sandwiches on Exotic Breads

The customer who asks for a ham and cheese on white must certainly be given the bread he expects, even if the plate is otherwise better enhanced. When an operation is merchandising specialty sandwiches, however, the bread itself can be made an important asset. Without becoming involved in on-premises baking, the operator can use commercially available breads that are more eye appealing than white, rye, and wheat: French and Italian loaves cut into sections or as small "rolls" stuffed from one end; pumpernickels of the Russian and Westphalian types; English muffins; Arab bread which has a pocket into which the sandwich filling is inserted; date and nut bread; and the various ethnic breads available from Greek, Hungarian, Italian, and German bakeries.

If on-premises baking is possible, using convenience doughs or primary ingredients, many attractive breads can be made, including cheese bread, frankfurter rolls with bits of relish, mustard bread, and various fruit breads.

Fancy Sandwiches and Canapés

Small fancy sandwiches in a variety of forms, and canapés, which are actually stylized, tiny, open-face sandwiches, have a minor role in catering service as cocktail party food. Occasionally, an à la carte restaurant offers a checkerboard sandwich if it expects the patronage of women shoppers or theatergoers, but these tea sandwiches seldom justify the labor they require if they cannot be made in quantity.

Pinwheel sandwiches These are made from day-old unsliced white bread cut the long way into thin slices or from canapé-sliced bread which is sold cut lengthwise. The crusts are trimmed, and then the bread is flattened with a rolling pin. It is coated with a spread or thin filling—strawberry jam, for example—and rolled from the narrow end tightly around a core of, for example, cream cheese, so that a compact cylinder is made. After being tied and wrapped in a moist towel, the roll is chilled and cut the next day into slices.

Checkerboard sandwiches A four-deck sandwich is made of crust-free alternate layers of wheat and white bread with a very thin filling (for example, dill butter on the wheat and smoked-salmon cream cheese spread on the white). The sandwich is cut into three slices, and the slices are rolled, with some filling between them, with the middle slice turned so that its first strip contrasts with the first strips of the slices above and below it. After the sandwich has been pressed together and chilled, it is cut again across the strips so that a checkerboard is made.

Mosaic sandwiches With canapé cutters, other specialty cutters, or even cookie cutters, identical shapes are cut from white and wheat bread. Then the pieces are shuffled and spread with thin filling, so that a round, fluted sandwich with a wheat bottom, a white middle layer, and a wheat top layer with a white insert can be made.

Envelopes and cornucopias A crust-free, thin slice of bread is folded, one diagonal corner to the other, and secured with a toothpick to form an envelope, or a cornucopia if one of the other corners is trimmed.

Roll-ups A thin slice of crustless bread is rolled around some solid filling (such as a small sausage) or a piece of ham is rolled around an asparagus spear, and then secured with a toothpick.

Canapés With a single slice of thin crustless bread approximately 1½ by 3 inches (the bread may be round, oval, or rectangular), a canapé consists of four parts: (1) the bread; (2) the coating on the bread (usually butter, which colors and protects it); (3) the main element which may be a solid slice (such as a piece of smoked salmon) or a paste (such as liver spread), and (4) the decoration. Most often, in institutional preparation, canapés are a mass production item. Canapé-sliced bread is either purchased or made by cutting thin lengthwise slices from an unsliced sandwich loaf. A compound butter is spread on the bread with a spatula, and then the main element is carefully laid down in the thinnest layer possible without leaving gaps in the bread. Then the edges are trimmed, including any pieces of the main element that hang over, and the canapés are evenly cut with a sharp knife or cutters. Then, without moving the pieces, each is decorated—perhaps with a bit of pickle or vegetable, a dab of topping from a pastry bag, or a cutout or fragment of meat or cheese. The topping is chosen to contrast with the main element: a sprig of dill on smoked salmon, for example, or a butter and mustard rosette and pickle chip on liver spread. If the canapés are evenly cut, several different kinds can be assembled into an attractive mosaic for a cocktail party tray.

Decorations and Garnishes for Sandwiches

Cold sandwiches can be enhanced by any of the eye-appealing garnishes and decorations suitable for cold plates. Items like pickles, vegetable garnishes, vegetable decorations with relishes, preserved fruits, and vegetable salads are certainly proper and attractive sandwich garnishes.

Several treatments seem especially well suited to making a sandwich more eye appealing, as they "correct" some of the sandwich's visual weaknesses. For example, the skewered garnish gives closed sandwiches the height that they lack. Toothpicks or inexpensive bamboo skewers can be used (items suggested should be used in the listed order from top to bottom of the skewer):

1 Marinated mushroom, black olive, pineapple chunk
2 Cheese ball, ham cube, midget gherkin
3 Cherry tomato, black olive, green stuffed olive, pickled onion
4 Radish rose, carrot curl, artichoke heart
5 Pickled cauliflower sprig, pineapple chunk, maraschino cherry

Flavored and colored butter is well suited to sandwiches made with pale bread. Without turning a ham and cheese sandwich into a birthday cake, one can decorate the cut edges with small rosettes. A large rosette of a dipping sauce on the plate lets the customer dunk the sandwich while he eats.

The top of the closed sandwich can be uplifted by some minor moisture-free garnish that suits the filling. For example, a row of overlapping red onion rings or crisscrossing, evenly cut pimiento rings adds visual appeal to an ordinary meat or meat and cheese sandwich.

Eye Appeal for Hot Foods

By the time a diner receives the hot food in many restaurant meals, he has had several drinks, cocktail nibbles, an appetizer, perhaps soup, relishes, bread and butter, and, sometimes as much salad as he can eat. He is not going to be very hungry. The appearance of his hot food, as it is placed before him, can renew his appetite. If it is unpleasant looking or merely of indifferent appearance, he will not be disposed to enjoy it. Hot foods cannot be a visual low point in the meal between attractive appetizers and spectacular salads or desserts; they must have strong eye appeal.

The problem of enhancing hot dishes has a further dimension: menu balance. Most of the expensive foods are attractive themselves—for example, sirloin steaks, lobster tails, or lamb chops—but for menu balance it is often necessary to include other cuts: ground or hashed meats, variety meats, or meats in sauces that are not particularly attractive. As some of them must be included, the restaurateur, except in a few steak and lobster houses, is often kept from using the simplest and most effective eye-appeal technique: a great-looking main element. A 16-ounce steak and a baked potato or a broiled lobster on an oversized platter, for example, will stimulate anyone's appetite, but what about the poached chicken, the sautéed liver, or the ground meat casserole dish?

Unlike the classic chef of the nineteenth century, the modern operator prepares mostly individual plates, not grand, ornate constructions with bases, armatures, mounts, dishes within dishes, and garnish upon garnish. He cannot easily hide unattractive foods under or in attractive ones. Rather, he must use techniques that result in an attractive total plate look that defuses the focus of the plate and makes the customer see the attractive elements, not the unattractive ones. His basic program of food enhancement might include five approaches:

1. Selectivity in the choice of items
2. Proper preparation techniques to present items at their best and to preserve their natural attractiveness
3. Strong accessorization for weak items
4. Eye-arresting garnishes
5. Finishing touches that unify the dish and bring it to its peak of attractiveness just before it is served

Selectivity in the Choice of Items

In American service, few items appear alone on the plate; meat is usually combined with vegetables and starches. In choosing items that will ultimately go together, care must be taken to balance color, texture, and form. Few cooks or restaurateurs, in choosing the daily vegetables and potatoes, ask themselves how these items will look with every menu item with which they might be combined.

In considering color, for example, the restaurateur or cook is dealing with whites (white meats, starches, and sauces); browns (brown meats, starches, and sauces); reds (tomato sauce and vegetables); yellows (hollandaise-based sauces and vegetables); and numerous vegetable colors (green, orange, beet red, etc.). They should be used skillfully. Certainly the most glaring errors, such as white sauce with white meat or browned vegetables with breaded meats, should be avoided.

Texture and form demand the same type of thinking. Will the plate look like 9 inches of hash, or are at least some of the elements solid looking? Will there be three mounds like so many bumps on a log, or do the items fit the plate and complement each other?

Once the restaurateur and the cook begin thinking of the overall plate look, their alternative choices are obvious: asparagus instead of peas with chicken croquettes, yellow instead of white rice with sliced turkey breast, and so on.

Proper Preparation

Visual appeal starts in the butcher shop and continues to the kitchen and service line. It is possible for an item to suffer visually at any point.

In the preparation of raw items, special attention should be given to trimming meat items attractively. Big margins of fat cover the plate, but they turn off customers. Fish are more attractive if the material in the head and gill sections is removed and the fins and tail are trimmed and reshaped. Birds and meats for roasting should be tied to facilitate even cooking and easy, attractive carving. Bone ends on fowls and chops should be scrupulously trimmed; flesh and the knuckles should be removed. Chicken and other fowl, when served whole or halved, should have the extremity of the wing, the tail, and the neck skin removed.

Proper cooking techniques furnish the key to eye appeal. Only a very dimly lit dining room will improve the visual appeal of gray broiled meats, olive-black green vegetables, lumpy mashed potatoes, burned fried foods, and curdled sauces.

The serving line has the same kind of pitfalls as poor cooking: If foods sit in a steam table or cool on a counter, they lose the fresh-cooked look that is so important to their appeal. The color and texture changes are even more obvious to the customer than the flavor changes.

Strong Accessorization

Items with an unattractive texture or form can be rescued by strong accessorization. A beef stew made from assorted oddments of beef looks much better as a closed beef pie in a casserole dish than as a hot plate. Meatballs threaded on a skewer with bits of colorful vegetables are more attractive than meat balls perched on a flat plate.

If the operation is purchasing fowl with parts missing, for example, ducklings, the ducks can be offered in pieces in orange sauce in a small bimetal pan, instead of as duckling for two.

There are enough attractive accessories available from both institutional and domestic suppliers to apply this approach to a number of items on the menu. The only limiting factor is the capacity of the dishroom to handle and store odd vessels. Consider serving chili in little black iron pots; corn beef hash in iron skillets; chicken à la king in ceramic chicken-shaped pots; mixed grills in wire grills; chicken or fish curry in a ceramic half coconut or pineapple; deep-fried, tempura-style vegetables family style in lacquer bowls; or fish sticks in a basket.

Eye-Arresting Garnishes

If the main element on a plate has an indifferent appearance—like an order of braised short ribs, for example—a dramatic garnish can make the plate exciting and, by extension, the short ribs as well.

Any cold garnish that will not melt (such as aspic timbales) can be used on a hot plate. Many oriental cuisines rely on this device for visual appeal: A stew may be served on fresh Bibb lettuce, or fresh sliced green onions may be scattered over it. There should be no hesitation about putting a cold item that will complement the flavor of the main element right on the plate with it.

Garnishes of this sort can range from greenery that is still green and does not resemble a maimed four-leaf clover—such as parsley, watercress, kale, chickory, grape leaves, or herb sprigs—to more elaborate vegetable vessels and decorations, pickles, preserved fruits, vegetable salads, and so on.

Hot garnishes can also be colorful, and they lend texture, height, and form to the plate as well. The following list offers suggestions.

1 Grilled whole tomatoes
2 Stuffed half tomatoes (with bread stuffings, vegetables in Mornay sauce, asparagus tips, etc.)
3 Artichoke bottoms filled with colorful vegetable purees or a harlequin arrangement of four quarters filled with different purees
4 Fried bread croutons in teardrop form with the round end dipped in chopped parsley
5 Turned broiled mushroom caps
6 Pastry tartlets filled with colorful vegetables or relishes
7 Vegetables turned to form barrels or balls, water-cooked or glazed with caramel made of butter and sugar
8 Potato boats with vegetable purees
9 Fried potatoes in attractive forms: souffle potatoes, gaufrette potatoes, shoestring potatoes
10 Vegetable cases—of zucchini, acorn squash, small pumpkins, small white eggplant—for the main element
11 Cases of bread or baked-goods for the main element: puff paste vol au vent, open tartlets, carved

and deep-fried bread "chests," or pastry or puff paste cutouts on top
12. Whole stuffed artichokes or onions
13. Fried eggs on top of the main element
14. Attractive, high, conical croquettes of any vegetables: corn, potatoes, spinach, etc.
16. Deep-fried or water-cooked pasta of any shape: Chinese noodles from vermicelli, or, also, bowties, shells, ribbons, tubes, angel's hair, etc.
17. Deep-fried potato flowers
18. Pureed vegetables forced through pastry bag tubes
19. Nuts: almonds in their many forms, walnuts, filberts, pecans, cashews, or pistachios
20. Sausages: small whole sausages, chunks, or grilled slices with frills
21. Rice molds made by pressing colored rice filled with bits of cooked vegetables in a butter timbale or other small mold
22. Deep-fried and tempura-fried (in light, transparent batter) vegetables: onion rings, peppers, pieces of green and yellow squash, or tomatoes
23. Crepes rolled around vegetable purees
24. Large, water-cooked macaroni filled with vegetables or meat purees from a pastry bag
25. Parsley deep-fried in very hot fat so that it crisps instantly
26. Dumplings, water-cooked, or water-cooked and then deep-fried

Finishing Touches

Some attention to details at the last moment can add considerable eye appeal. For example, even a handsome well-broiled steak is enhanced by a light glaze of butter just before it is given to the waiter. Some operations make a compound butter—often of butter, red pepper sauce, and chopped parsley—freeze it in a long star mold or piped in rosettes from a pastry bag, and place these frozen pieces on the steak as it leaves the kitchen, so that some butter melts over the steak.

An au gratin treatment also enhances many meat, sauce, and vegetable preparations. The cook sprinkles either bread crumbs and butter or bread crumbs and grated cheese over the article and browns it in the broiler or salamander. Clarified brown butter livens up vegetables that have languished too long in the steam table or pot. A garnish of a few exquisitely cut vegetables, cooked until just tender, in the customer's bowl makes any soup seem freshly prepared. Plates and platters that lack unity can be given a feeling of completeness by adding a border of mashed potatoes or a stiff vegetable puree forced through a pastry bag. The border can then be browned.

Added Eye Appeal for Cakes, Desserts, and Beverages

Cakes, desserts, and beverages are already eye appealing. If they are not, they are such disasters that no artifice will redeem them. Therefore, any effort at decoration by a restaurateur is really an effort to establish distinction. Splendid cakes, delicious desserts, and fine beverage products are available to everyone. The restaurateur tries to make the quality convenience cheese cake, the foolproof sponge cake from the mix, the strawberry ice cream, or the name-brand rum and name-brand daiquiri mix his own by adding some original visual accent.

Cakes

The operation with a baker that can make a cake completely from scratch needs no guidance in cake decorating: If the man can bake it, he can decorate it. On the other hand, many operators purchase cakes or sophisticated cake mixes without really realizing that the one thing they cannot purchase—custom decoration—can be accomplished without highly skilled personnel.

At least three on-premises convenience approaches are possible: (1) decorating with fruit; (2) decorating with add-ons, or (3) decorating with pastry bags and tubes.

Decorating with Fruit

Plain cakes, either made from a mix or purchased, can be decorated with canned or plain fruit. Fresh peach slices, for example, can be soaked in sugar water to prevent discoloration, drained, and then carefully shingled over the top of the cake. Canned fruit—for example, pitted cherries—is equally easy to use. The syrup is heated, thickened with a little cornstarch or gelatin dissolved in cold liquid, cooled, and then spread with the fruit over the cake.

Decorating with Add-Ons

A number of add-on decorations and garnishes for cakes are readily available. Even the sugar flowers and frills that decorate wedding cakes can be purchased completely made.

The operator might also consider completely prepared icings in a multitude of colors and flavors and the numerous decorations with which he can top them for a custom look: flower petals, sprinkles, chopped or slivered nuts, candied violets and roses, chopped dried and candied fruit, chocolate chips, peppermint candies, coconut, sweet breakfast cereals, marshmallows, and so on.

The supply houses for professional bakers will also sell him special stencils with which he can apply cocoa powder or chocolate powder to make a painting.

Individual portions of cake can be given eye appeal and flavor interest with fountain syrups and ingredients such as crushed pineapple, strawberries, and maple nuts.

Decorating with a Pastry Bag and Tube

The complicated wedding cake constructions of icing are difficult, but there are many simpler decorative designs that are attainable after half an hour's experimentation.

It is certainly worthwhile experimenting because the equipment and materials—a few yards of parchment paper and a beginner's set of metal pastry tubes—cost only a few dollars.

Figure 10.1 indicates how a paper pastry bag is made. Paper bags are preferable to cloth because several can be made, each for a different icing, and they are sanitary and disposable. Beginners should make two paper bags: Fill one with icing, cut the top from it, and insert the tube over the hole. Then, place the second one over the first so that the tip is sandwiched between them.

At that point, with a prepared icing or frosting in the bag, the cook is ready to decorate. Plain tubes will let him make lines, letters, and borders. Star tubes, which are the most frequently used, allow flower forms (rosettes) and decorative, straight, and curved lines. Combination leaf and border tubes permit ridged leaves, ornate borders, and fantasy flowers.

If first efforts are simple, carefully planned, and perhaps practiced on a piece of laminated plastic sheeting the size of the cake, the results are surprising.

Desserts

Desserts can be enhanced in much the same ways as cakes. A wide variety of quality convenience items is available: canned fruits, ice cream, sherbet, ready-to-eat and easy-to-make puddings, and the like. To them, the operator can add other convenience items—fresh fruits, any of the add-on items suggested for cakes (above), liqueurs, and whipped toppings—for

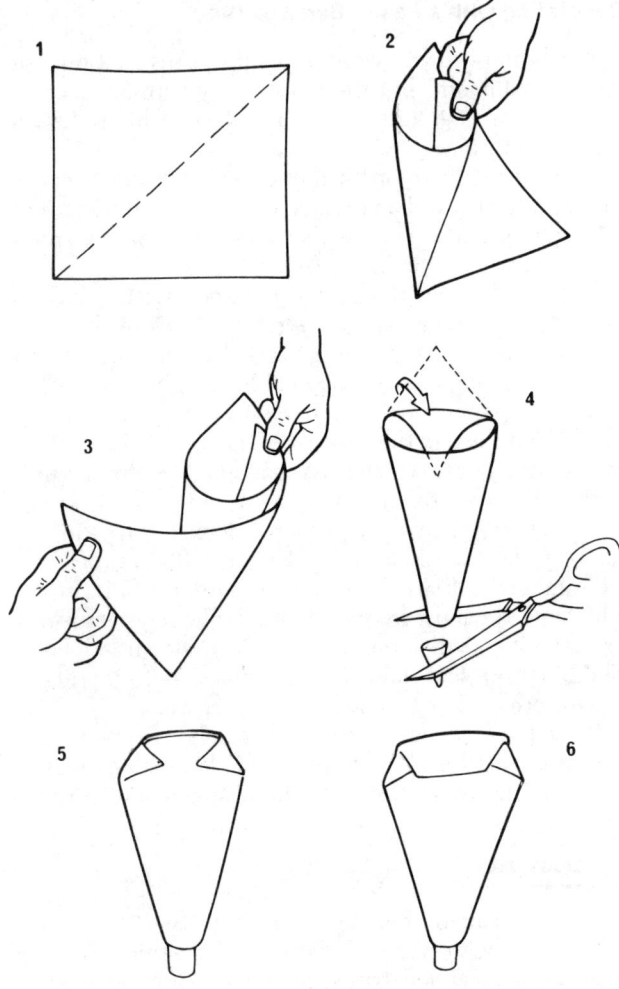

Figure 10.1. The above diagram shows a paper pastry bag in the making. A metal pastry tube fits into the opening left when the pointed end is removed.

original results. If he considers color, is adventurous in his choice of ingredients, and invests in some dramatic accessorization, his creations will have uniqueness and eye appeal.

For example, starting with an hourglass-shaped wine glass on a long stem, first pour a teaspoon of cassis (black currant) liqueur in the bottom. Then fill the glass half full with vanilla ice cream. Add a ¾-inch layer of canned blueberry turnover filling (the pieces are bigger than pie filling), a 1-inch layer of pistachio ice cream, some frozen sliced strawberries, and enough extra vanilla ice cream to fill the glass within ¾ inch of the top. Sprinkle the top with crushed peanut brittle, and then add a rosette or a teaspoon of whipped cream. Finally, shred semi-sweet chocolate over the whole confection. Up to the whipped cream step, the dessert can be made in quantity and stored in a vertical freezer. It looks sensational and quite obviously there is a pleasant surprise in almost every bite—all with little cost and effort.

Consider using chocolate pudding, rum, and canned pears; diluted raspberry jam, peach halves, and strawberry ice cream; canned chestnuts in syrup, vanilla ice cream, and candied violets; or a canned baked apple with orange liqueur and chocolate chips.

Beverages

Any beverage—hot or cold, alcoholic or nonalcoholic—profits from strong accessorization: unusual glasses, distinctive cups and mugs, and unique serving pitchers all add interest.

As most beverages are attractive, or at least not unattractive, an effort at increasing their eye appeal is generally limited to garnishing the glass or cup. For example, alcoholic beverages and fruit drinks, which are commonly garnished with a slice of lemon or a wedge of lime, can be embellished by using a decorated plastic toothpick as a skewer threaded with a variety of fruits:

1. Lemon wedge, strawberry, and green maraschino cherry
2. Orange slice, red maraschino cherry, and chunk of pineapple
3. Mint sprig, white grapes, and small apricot half
4. Half kumquat, prune pickled in brandy, and piece of preserved ginger
5. Small orchid, quarter of lime, and small pickled pear

A "Bloody Mary" can be made more interesting by using a stick of celery or a scallion as a stirrer, and a lime, lemon, and radish skewer pick.

Glasses for cocktails made with sugar can be frosted by dipping the rim of the glass in lemon juice or egg white and then in superfine sugar. Or, they may really be frosted by freezing or using a carbon dioxide frosting machine where its use is legal.

Milk drinks, such as milk shakes and ice cream sodas, can be further glamorized with colored whipped cream. This is made easily by adding food coloring or syrup, instead of sugar, to cream in a canister-type whipped cream "charger." The whipped cream itself can be sprinkled with tinted coconut, crumbled peanut brittle, shredded chocolate, sprinkles, and all sorts of other goodies.

Instead of floating unadorned fruit slices in punch, the restaurateur/caterer might consider any of the fruit decorations suggested earlier, such as notched citrus fruits, fruit crowns, cutouts, or orange peel roses made like tomato roses. The creation could be completed with colored ice cubes or fresh fruit frozen in a block of ice by the ice house (which can keep it clear).

Again, the better it looks, the better it will taste.